To Brown,

Love Jud & Kathy

Dangerous Fathers,
Problem Mothers,
and Terrible Teens

Dangerous Fathers,
Problem Mothers,
and Terrible Teens

CARLYLE MARNEY

ABINGDON PRESS

NEW YORK   NASHVILLE

DANGEROUS FATHERS, PROBLEM MOTHERS, AND TERRIBLE TEENS

Copyright © MCMLVIII by Abingdon Press

Library of Congress Catalog Card Number: 58-5390

The lines on the dedication page are from Robert Frost, "The Death of the
Hired Man," and are used by permission of the publishers, Henry Holt and Co.,
Inc.

B

SET UP, PRINTED, AND BOUND BY THE
PARTHENON PRESS, AT NASHVILLE,
TENNESSEE, UNITED STATES OF AMERICA

HOME

    is the place
where,
       when you have to go there,
they have to take you in.

CONTENTS

ANY MAN'S FAMILY

Character's the Thing

I NEVER WILL BE A MATHEMATICIAN. IT TOOK ME THREE TRIES TO PASS high-school algebra; but I do remember what an axiom is. It is a proposition or a principle, based on experience, to which people in general agree. Without being mathematical about it at all, I begin this family discussion with an axiom: *Family training never can rise above family character.* Character is the thing. If it is bad it will always reveal itself, even in the most plush circumstances. If it is good it will always demonstrate itself as good, even in the poorest surroundings. Character is the thing. A family in its training never can rise beyond its character.

We give our children many opportunities and try to teach them many things. Added to the things all teachers teach are all the special disciplines. Some of these are more or less imposed on unwilling sufferers: usually special skills the parents did not acquire. Stubby little girls squirm through ballet lessons; short-handed little boys frustrate themselves through the first agonies of piano-dom. Everything from horseback to pipe organ, from plug-fishing to philosophy, is part of our attempts to make our children become what we never have become. And all the time the basic family relationship that makes a family a family is not taught. It is caught. And the level of the family never really rises beyond its character.

Like yeast in dough, the family's basic character works in and through the life of each member.

Now it should be obvious that from both within and without the family has enemies. But I can think of no enemy the family has that is not basically and fundamentally a character enemy. For the only place a family can really be destroyed is in terms of its character, for the family is essentially a moral relationship. That is to say, it is in the highest sense of the word a religious relationship. Even when it is a bad relationship, it is still a bad *religious* relationship, for the family is basically and fundamentally a moral relationship. All its enemies are moral enemies. Whether the enemy be selfishness, or some other form of self-centeredness, unworthy ambition, or social pride, or whether it be something more tangible like the demands of a man's job, or civic responsibilities, or the industrial machine—whatever it be that works against a family, the damage is done in the realm of the moral, and is, therefore, a character enemy. All your family enemies are character enemies.

But the character can be changed. The character of the whole family can be changed. The family character is determined by what the family considers to be valuable. The character determinant is the sense of value when a family is able to elevate its sense of what is valuable; the character automatically rises to a new level.

What do you count to be important at your house? A certain social position? Your family's character is automatically determined by your judgment of the worth of social position. Professional standing, a certain credit rating, the acquisition of a pile of things—do you count one of these to be the most valuable? Then your family's character is automatically determined at a rather low level. Or do you find your family's main interest centering in the rearing of real men and women, development of healthy minds and bodies, the growth of gracious spirits? Your family character is already determined, and lies at a comparatively high level. Character is determined by the sense of the valuable.

All of this is to say that the end product of a family's training is always a precise picture of the family's character. At least it is so in my experience. Let a story show you what I mean.

It was obvious that the lady was in great distress. She was wringing her hands and on the verge of tears. Other members of her family shifted back and forth from foot to foot, managing to look very hungry and quite downcast about the whole business. They had come hundreds of miles from home to see the Board of Parole about their kinsman. Unable to secure his release from prison they wanted me to give them money to get home. Since I am one of those fellows who believes most anything anybody says, I asked our administrator to send the whole family home. But Bill is wiser than I in such matters. When he bought the bus tickets he wrote on the back of the cashier's stub, "Refund should be made only to the purchaser," and signed his name. Ten days or so later came a bus-company check refunding the amount we had spent for the tickets. With the check was a copy of a letter sent to the family for whom we had bought the tickets saying that the bus company could not make refund except to the purchaser since he had requested that any refund be paid to him.

I guess I never will learn—the only thing true about the mournful story I had heard had been the son's prison sentence. These people had gone home in their own car, then attempted to cash the tickets they had squirmed and dodged from us. I wonder if they really were surprised when their kinsman was denied parole? Poor kid, he had never had a chance with a family character like that. He must have learned early to squirm and dodge his way through life.

Family training in its end product never rises above its character.

Time Is the Enemy

SOME OF THE FAMILY'S WEAKNESSES ARE INHERENT IN ITS OWN make-up. Not all its enemies are outside, some are within the framework. A great family weakness is its transitoriness. The time of our association as a family goes by so fast.

As an institution, the family is very, very old. As an association of individuals, it is very, very temporary. The rate at which a family ages is fearfully rapid. Yesterday she cut her first tooth, today she cut a twelve-year molar, and tomorrow you are ordering a new upper plate for yourself. Time goes by, and in a family he becomes our enemy. Maybe my friend was wiser than he knew when he let his eldest drag her little B-B gun along through the brush on early morning deer-hunts with him. I guess he knew time was an enemy and that in just a matter of weeks she would be sleeping until eleven on Saturday mornings and dreaming about formals and perfumes and other things completely feminine.

Time is an enemy and a father has to get what he has with his children fast. But if time is the enemy of the family, if the family's weakness is its transitoriness, there is a reason. And that reason usually is our preoccupation with ourselves. Once more, our sense of what is really valuable determines what happens to our family. I speak as a father to say that when a father's great concern is himself, or his work, or his calling, or his opportunities, then time has gotten in some deadly blows before he knows it, and some opportunities are gone that will never return. But what can a man do? He has obligations, he has a job, he has a calling, there are demands made on him—what can he do to put his hands on time and turn him into a docile helper instead of a stern and unrelenting enemy?

Of course there are obligations, and callings, and opportunities, and if a man survives in this hurly-burly world, he has to take some of them. But what can he do? He can split-up and double-up. He can do part of one thing in order to have time to do all of another. He can put first things where they belong.

Again, a story will illustrate what I mean: The first half of the Villanova game was not too sharp. The boys looked pretty good and there was some nice blocking and tackling, but it was awfully hot and the game was not too tight. At the half a tall fellow and a tiny little blond girl about four or five years old claimed the seats next to us. And although the second half was quite a ball game, I found myself watching the little girl almost as much as I watched the game. She was not at all concerned as to who had the ball. The score meant nothing. The roaring excitement around us did not divert her. She was wholly occupied with a series of grape-flavored snow-cones and the important business of carrying on a conversation with her father. Something was happening between those two that was really worth seeing. One got the impression that it was quite a bit more important than what was happening in the arena below. I saluted the Governor that afternoon to myself, because he had pushed aside a lot of things to make time his friend by bringing his tiny little lady to eat her snow-cones with her daddy at the last half of a football game. How make time your friend? Come in at the half on some very important matters, by refusing to be a slave to a date book.

A classic example of this is the great mother of Charles and John Wesley. In the days long before there were any real helps to make a day lighter and less long, eighteen children came to the home of Suzanna Wesley and her husband. I have understood it was her lifelong habit within her own family to make a little while each day for each child. I doubt if she knew or thought much about which of her brood would become immortal, but John and Charles Wesley are men among millions. Suzanna's refusal to let time become her enemy doubtless has more to do with this fact than the later years John and Charles Wesley spent at Oxford University.

How keep time from being an enemy, how make him a friend? Mark through some pages ahead in your obligation book. Make a date you mean to keep with some very important persons to do some mighty unimportant things that have some tremendous consequences. Do like old Joshua—reach up and stop the sun while you enjoy the family God gave you. It changes as fast as the earth travels.

Self-Discipline Is an Obligation

FAMILY FAILURES CAN BE LAID AT SOME FUNDAMENTAL POINT TO the matter of a lack of discipline. The family's fatal failure occurs when it fails to teach its individual members self-discipline.

Sometimes other institutions really do a better job of teaching self-discipline than the most cozy of family relationships. I noticed this especially last week in connection with my visit to a fine home for dependent children. I was met at the door by a lovely little fairy of a girl about three and a half years old. She and her matron-mother were the only ones at home; all the rest of the youngsters in that cottage were at school. So it was my delightful privilege to be escorted through the rooms where some eighteen children make their home, by the little sister of the whole house. I was amazed at her knowledge of the family routine and by her own self-assurance and discipline in matters concerning her own possessions. The high light of the whole trip for her was to take me into the room she shared with two older girls and show me her own "Sunday shoes." I couldn't help contrasting the perfect order with which a three-and-a-half-year-old child had learned to keep her own possessions with the disorder of things in most of our little-girl closets in homes that are sometimes thought to be more fortunate. And I couldn't help wondering if the self-discipline the little child had already gotten wouldn't make of her a far more stable person than would be produced in some of the more affluent homes I have known.

Where do we modern parents begin these failures in self-discipline? We begin to fail to teach self-discipline when we waste the opportunities of babyhood: I have a book in hand—written over a hundred years ago. It still is a top-notch volume in the field of family relations. It is Horace Bushnell's famous book, *Christian Nurture*. Buy it. Buy it just for pages 200-212, if for no other reason. Read for yourself and see how far ahead of his time Dr. Bushnell was a hundred years ago when he began to claim that children are damaged more in the nursing months than anyone has ever dreamed. Read, and then remember for yourself what powers are turned loose through baby indulgence and what discipline in a human life is forever denied by some kinds of parental pampering.

As a boy, I thought the many tales I read of the rigor of the boyhood of the American Indian a tough story indeed. I am beginning to learn now that what the Indian tribe was seeking was a disciplined adulthood for each of its members.

Life will impose a discipline when the family fails in this matter of self-discipline. Life itself can so bind and frustrate an individual with the disciplines it wraps around him that every conceivable kind of brokenness, neurosis, maladjustment, and frustration walks the streets of every city.

Nor can you expect schoolteachers, scoutmasters, and football coaches to make up the difference. Who could ever estimate the moral value of a real schoolteacher? Who could put a price tag on the contribution of a devoted and able scoutmaster? And, in my own case, I shall never be able to say what the moral worth of the contribution of two football coaches has been. But none of these can make up the difference resulting from a family failure in self-discipline.

The fact remains that childhood indulgence can issue in a vapid sensualism that finds its only support eventually in alcohol or dope. Procrastination in matters of family discipline can produce an individual that seems to be will-less and witless. Preoccupation with matters of less concern usually will issue in the production of grown men and women who somehow are never quite able to focus on life's more worthy meanings.

Families must be brought to recognize that the opportunity is immediate and the younger the child the greater the opportunity; that every worthy community institution is an ally in the matter of teaching self-discipline; and that the necessity for learning self-discipline runs all the way through society.

Maybe you would like some practical suggestions on how to go about inducing the development of self-discipline in your own youngsters. I am seeking such for myself and have come up with four or five ideas I am finding to be worthy: teach orderliness; give responsibility; expect help; induce management; develop trust, then trust them.

The family has failed when its individual members have not been led into a life that is characterized by self-discipline.

What They Can Afford to Want

ON THE BACK PAGE OF A LITTLE MAGAZINE THAT COMES TO ME A friend of mine always writes a personal letter to his customers. This month's Christmas letter concerned the first letter he had ever written—a letter to Santa Claus in which a-six-year-old boy had shared with Santa Claus his own wants and desires. Now I know the man pretty well who wrote this letter, and even before he wrote that first letter to Santa Claus, someone had done a good job on him. They had taught him *what he could afford to want*. Thousands of letters have gone out since that first letter to Santa Claus. There are not many countries nor kinds of business into which letters from this man have not gone. He learned years ago that work is the joy of putting out, that work is the joy of producing; work is not the joy of getting, which is incidental. Someone did a good job on his "wanter."

It is the responsibility of parents to teach children what they can afford to want. All of us, especially adults, have a "gimme" inside of us. It gets out of whack and goes crazy sometimes unless we have a proper scale of value.

Parents err. We give too much, too many, too little, and too long. And every Christmastime we complain about how poorly the things we give our children are put together. "Toys are too flimsy nowadays," we say; "they are not put together right." And we all know that there are lots of things in today's living that are not put together right. It is the sin of parental indulgence that creates a market for such.

But I have in my study a toy that's put together right. It is an old birch stick with a moose-hide thong on the end of it attached with a homemade nail to a piece of wood shaped crudely with an axe to look like an Indian canoe. It must be at least fifty years old, and at least that long ago some little Indian boy pulled it up and down the banks of the Oskalaneo River in northern Canada. In an old abandoned Indian camp in the ruins of what had once been home, it had stayed together half a century. There were five or six old muzzle-loading rifles with the stocks completely gone and the muzzles rusted almost beyond recognition. There were piles of rotted clothing and the abandoned utensils of an Indian camp. The boy for whom it was made is long since dead of t.b. or smallpox or a bear, but his little toy is still as usable as it was fifty years ago. It was made of the right stuff; it was put together right!

That is to say, it was made out of things that were at hand in the shape of something he could afford to want.

In every home I know the material is at hand, if parents would use it—the stuff of human relations within a family out of which love and intelligence can shape things a child can afford to go on wanting all through adulthood. Teach your child what he can afford to go on wanting. It is a family job, and it can begin at Christmastime, even with toys.

Inconsequential Gods

SOME OF YOU ARE ALWAYS GRIEVED OVER WHAT YOU CANNOT DO AT Christmastime. You know already that your children will be disappointed, because you have taught them to want what they can't afford to want, because already they are beginning to learn to worship the inconsequential. Others of you, a little more affluent, will try with one grand splurge of buying to atone for all you haven't done through the rest of the year. And not only parents, but also grandparents are busy trying to buy for their grandchildren things they couldn't afford for their own. This is a seasonal symptom of our worship of the fragmentary. This is one way we enthrone the partial. Bad judgment is involved in worshiping an inconsequential god. Dangerous and unworthy business makes us miss the main thing badly.

In the hotel lobby, a thousand miles from home, I came across a grand old friend. We talked for hours and somewhere along he told me of the death of one who had been very dear to him. The old man whose death he described had come to maturity in a section where the discovery of oil had changed the whole economy of the country. In the midyears of his life he had taken advantage of all that was going on around him and had advanced from carpenter to storekeeper to man of wealth and possessions. Then a subtle change began to come over him in his older years and he became an avid grasper after money and more money. His motto became, "Cash on the barrelhead." No man could owe him anything long. As his love for money increased, his regard for family, church, friends, society, and everything else, declined in proportion. So it was that some years before his death he lost his church, he lost his God, he lost his friends, he lost his family, and at the moment of his death one grown son said to his sister, "Did you see the hate in your daddy's eyes when he died?" My friend who was telling the story stopped for a moment. His mind floated back to the time when he first met the man whom we were discussing—the first years of his adulthood when he had been a good craftsman, doing good work in a good shop. And he said to me, by way of closing the story, "He was the best saw filer I ever saw."

Some obituary, some epitaph—"the best saw filer I ever saw."

When either parent worships the fragmentary, it is fatal to the family. When either father or mother enthrones in life something that is only partial, then the whole life develops an off-centeredness that throws the family off base.

What if, by dint of your own skill, devotion to your work, sacrifice of human values, and all the rest it costs, you do become the best lawyer in your city? The chances are ninety-nine to nothing you will have lost your family and most everything else that is really precious to you in achieving it. What if you are queen of the flower show, or head of the woman's club, or the champion bridge-player, or even the most active "saint" at church, if you lose your family as a price of achievement?

What if by sacrifice of time, health, energy, and all that is holy you do become the best salesman in your whole territory? It may have cost you more than you can afford to enthrone the professional in the center of your life. People were not meant to enthrone the professional. The personal is meant to be on the throne in the center of a man's life. The familial is meant to be central for both father and mother.

What if, through the loss of everything that is really important to you, you do become the ranking physician in your territory? What if you are the best sawfiler anybody ever saw? It is not worth it at the cost of everything truly personal and truly important in living.

It is tremendously important to be a good craftsman at whatever one's craft may be, but I still insist that the craft of parenthood is more important than any of the others. And the social graces go a long way in helping mamma help papa make it. But the grace of parenthood is primary in both importance and worth! Parents have to figure out what they are going to worship, and they had best not worship an inconsequential god. All these things are important: the law, sales, the medical profession, ministry—they all serve humanity in some sense or another, but they also can miss humanity at its most important center. There are a thousand ways a mother can go to give herself to the surrounding community needs, but these ways are also avenues through which evil pride can wreck her most important personal relationships.

So you are better off if you are not putting too much emphasis on the inconsequential. You are better off if you are not trying with one grand splurge to atone for all you haven't done the rest of the year. It is good when the center of family life is not

in the inconsequential. Let the fragmentary remain a fragment.
Keep the main thing where it belongs.

Everybody's Doing It

A RIDICULOUSLY INVALID SCALE OF MEASURE FOR A FAMILY'S ACTION
is wrapped up in the phrase most every family I know has at
some time heard from one or another of its members. It has
particular effectiveness as a weapon in the hands of an adolescent
child: "Why not, Mother? Everybody is doing it."

Some time ago a digest of the work of the great Harvard
sociologist, Pitirim Sorokin, appeared in *Time* magazine. Dr.
Sorokin insists that we must test a thing by our own conscience.
We must ask if it will harm the community; if it will harm our
family; if it will harm ourselves. A certain way of life may not
be right even if ninety per cent of the neighbors are doing it.

There are areas where the family simply must not succumb
to the strategy so often quoted that says because everybody is
doing it, it must be all right. For example, it is simply not right
for a family to live by the "everybody is doing it" motto in
connection with the use of its own income. Again, the "everybody is doing it" routine is no adequate guide in controlling
and rearing of children. Such a guide is positively immoral if
it is used to control our behavior patterns. Least of all is the
phrase "everybody is doing it" a fit motto to determine whether
or not a family worships together. There is in our time still room
and also deep need in this world for family individualities.

I am not unaware of what tremendous power the motto "everybody is doing it" has with teen-agers. In those early adolescent
years in particular there exists in most every personality a

desperate need to belong. And to belong involves having certain kinds of clothes, being able to go certain places, having a certain kind of house, having certain furnishings, making a living in a certain kind of way; it involves being able to have a certain amount of pride in a family along purely materialistic lines, and so on, and so on. I know fathers driven frantic by the pressure from their own adolescent children to "keep up." There are times when a family must say simply, "We can't afford this," or "We just don't do that," or "This is a thing our family just does." These things have to be said even when such a way of life may be contrary to the actions and attitudes of the whole neighborhood. For the simple fact remains that what even our whole culture does is not necessarily a good safeguard for the individual family, because whole cultures become decayed and dying.

In the final analysis, your great bulwark for the continued lifetime of your own family rests within your own family. The family is the basic unit. It is true that such a way of life as I am suggesting may isolate it from its neighbors, but the family exists only as long as it is strong principled with a kind of rightness. I was talking with a friend of mine, a research physicist on the coast, a man who would not ordinarily use religious terminology. We were talking about how families can get together and stay together, and I was gratified and amused that, in trying to express himself, he was forced to use a definitely religious term. "Why," he said, "What I am speaking of is a kind of righteousness." A family has to feel within itself the innate rightness in what it does, even if it goes contrary to the whole neighborhood—which brings us back to Sorokin's paragraph in *Time* magazine that I referred to above. The family has to test by its own conscience.

But you may well ask a second question. How can a family

get started on such a way of life? Organize a family council. You may never have had one. It ought to include every member of the family, even the youngsters too young as yet to talk. Everyone in it ought to be present because everyone in it needs to be considered. Let the father or the mother, or the oldest child, or each member of the family, state the problem as he sees it—whatever it is that confronts this particular family. Then let the members consider all solutions together. Pick the best one and stick to it, even if it makes you stick out in your neighborhood like a sore thumb.

A Family Inventory

SOME TIME AGO IN THE "NEW YORKER" THERE APPEARED A 77-WORD short story. I haven't been able to forget it. Up in Summit, New Jersey, a six-year-old lad who had just learned how to count asked his mother what was the last, last, very last number he could count. The mother answered that he could count, and count, and count, but he could never, never, never count the last number. She turned away thinking how neatly she had slipped the concept of infinity into the mind of a little boy, but when she turned back to him, he was lying on his bed softly weeping.

Sixty-year-olds do it too. We spend our whole lives trying to get to the last number we can count, only to be frustrated as the concept of infinity begins to dawn on us. In the family this desire to acquire the last number that can be acquired takes on a kind of frenzy—a frenzy to have, to get, to own, to be. How about turning back and counting what you have already got?

1. Have you got a wife (or a husband) who has made it a habit to keep personal attractiveness at its very best?

25

2. Have you the habit of eliminating the needless irritants and sources of antagonism? Have you started stopping the little annoying things that get on each other's nerves?

3. Have you quit cherishing feelings of resentment? That is, have you learned to forgive and forget? Have you stopped bringing up things that have been once settled?

4. Do you keep looking for new ways to do joyful things together? Have you kept the spirit of courtship and romance? Have you refused to neglect each other simply because children have come? Have you remembered that your ties will last long after they have left home? Do you remember the importance of little courtesies?

5. Have you learned to be loyal? That is to say, have you refused to talk about faults or troubles to outsiders? And have you learned not to criticize or joke embarrassingly before your friends? Have you learned to be partners in every sense of the word?

6. Have you quit wondering what would have happened if you had married someone else? Do you know by now that such daydreams do no good?

7. Have you learned that neither can really dominate the other? And surely, by the end of six months of marriage, both of you should have learned not to get mad at the same time.

8. How long has it been since you have tried to get your way by unfair means? If you have a husband or a wife who will never use an unfair means to get his or her way, you are pretty close to having a marriage.

9. Have you learned how often the impulse to criticize comes from dissatisfaction with yourself? Have you analyzed what dissatisfaction with self can do to a family relationship in terms of hypercriticism, nagging, and the unneeded punishment of children?

10. And, the saving grace of more than one marriage, have you kept your sense of humor?

11. Are you sure your partner knows he is first in your life? This is basic. It appears especially in dealing with in-laws, outside interests, professional concerns, financial worries, and the thousand-and-one competitive urges that press against the modern family.

12. Can you honestly say that you think you have learned to make the best of whatever life brings?

13. Have you made together a long-range plan of finances?

14. Have you quit neglecting your health?

15. What are you doing to cultivate your own spiritual life?

All these things, in one way or another, point to this last thing: Have you learned that every real marriage is an eternal triangle? It is the heart of the Christian doctrine of marriage—this *man* and this *woman* and the *God*. In some lectures on the family, Theodore Adams referred to Rodin's great figure of a gigantic hand with a man and a woman standing in the palm of it. In your own marriage have you the sense that you and your best-loved one stand within the providential love and care of a personal God?

The best way I know to stop the frenzied desire to win the frustrating combat with the infinity of things one does not possess, is a solemn, sobersided analysis of the tremendous values you do have.

A long time ago, with less than enough money for a month's groceries, as bride and groom, we entered on a six-year course of graduate study in a seminary. Although our financial condition improved somewhat as the years went by, there just wasn't any extra money for anything. Most of the time, when the insurance had been paid and the groceries had been bought, there wasn't even the price of a movie in the house. I don't remember how long I went without buying even a sock—fortunately I had a pair or two. And it is amazing how long a trousseau can be made to serve without replacement. But we discovered a thing that has blessed our whole lives: The richest things a husband and wife can know—God's choicest gifts—have no price tag on them. They are absolutely free. They are here right in the middle of life for the taking, for the enjoying, for the using, for the knowing. We came to know friends—friends of the long road. And in moments when the pressure of our work would let us, we learned how free air is, and how wonderful God's fresh sunlight is, and how amazing his nature is. Life begins to have a rich, free music of its own when you acquire the proper evaluation of what you have got and look around you for what is free for the taking.

They Shall Be One Flesh

SOMEONE SAID SOMEWHERE, "ALL POLITICAL ANARCHY BEGINS WITH domestic anarchy." That is to say, there is no widespread lawlessness that can come to a society or state that is not preceded by the breakdown of the home structure of that society. We are talking about what marriage should be, and always is, when it is really marriage.

Marriage is a separation. Several places in the Scripture does it say, "For this cause [marriage] shall a man leave his father and mother." In one of the psalms the injunction is plain: "Forget also thine own people, and thy father's house." That is to say, marriage is a separation from the place of sonship in order that there might be the creation of a new place as husband and father.

28

Marriage is not only a separation, it is a devotement. The scripture goes on to say, "and cleave to his wife." There comes with the creation of each new home a new center of interest, love and affection, or there is no home. Marriage is separation and devotement. But marriage is also a union. Jesus himself said, "If they are one how can they be two again." Ideally, marriage is a submersion of two partial selves into the creation of one whole self. The male finds in the female the rest of himself, and certainly the reverse is true. This trilogy is always present in true marriage: separation, devotement, and union. "For better, for worse, for richer, for poorer, in sickness and in health," we say, and then add, "and I will keep myself only unto thee so long as we both shall live." Fidelity that appears in true marriage is always a matter of separation, devotement, and union.

I have said that all enemies of the family in the marriage relation are character enemies. This marriage union, made up of separation, devotement, and oneness, has only three real enemies. The first one is an insider—yourself. The things a man's preoccupation with himself can do to a family are almost beyond belief. All selfishness, all pride, all preoccupation, work unbelievable havoc within the family relationship. The second great enemy is an outsider—that is to say, any other. When any other interest, concern, or person presses its way into the life of the family as having more worth than the family relationship itself, then the family relationship becomes less and less a religious affair—that is to say, less and less a matter of concern between concerned personalities and more and more a simple social incidentalism.

But the third enemy is one to which we particularly address ourselves. He is neither insider nor outsider. This enemy is a besider. He lives alongside you in many instances—sometimes in the same house. And even in a distant city he can work harm. This besider is the family you were supposed to have forsaken in essence when you created your own home. The besider is your own childhood family—the in-laws of the one you married. Your family. Let me make some candid suggestions about how to meet this prospective destructive force within the family. Strange, you say, that I would call one of the greatest relationships for good within the family's potential a destructive force, but it can be a most destructive force. Your family, the family with which you grew up, must find its proper place with respect to your own new family, or you are in for stormy days ahead. Let me give some pointers. These pointers are directed to keeping the proper relationship between any man and his in-laws, between any wife and her husband's family:

The respective faults and demerits of your respective families are not fit subject for your discussion. There are things about the in-laws that both husband and wife must ignore. The background of your marriage partner is not subject to your inspection or continued criticism. The idiosyncrasies and eccentricities of your partner's family are not fit subjects for even a teasing conversation.

The occasional or casual needs of your partner's family are not occasions for jealousy or feelings of neglect. Men are still sons as long as their parents live. Wives are still daughters as long as the parents are alive. We are all subject to filial laws, and the needs of our particular childhood families are not to be occasions of ill will in our own family. In case of serious and prolonged need on the part of one family or the other, the situation must be accepted with grace and love and understanding. In instances where the families must live together, it should always be clear whose home it is. This calls for great tact, and sometimes for forthrightness.

The absolute essential in getting along with besiders is respect. The basic attitude that must be maintained between in-laws and younger families is one of mutual loyalty. The greatest good comes from a positive demonstration of mutual trust. The most needed attitude is one of adulthood. The greatest blessing that comes from the right family relationship is that no one ever need feel cut off from the other. This issues in the joy of real family communion.

Sometimes older parents have to learn the virtue of with-holding help from their struggling youngsters in their new married relationship. Always older parents must learn the willingness to release their own children to find not only the heartaches and agonies of the married relationship, but the great victories and marvelous blessings that it brings.

Younger parents must learn the proper attitude to have when accepting help from their older parents. And they must learn, too, the peculiar joy that comes in having the privilege of making a place for themselves.

When all these enemies are faced—the insider, the outsider, and the besider—there issues in every family built on separation, devotement, and union, a united front. This united front that makes a family a family usually will demonstrate first that both father and mother in the young family have experienced death of self in their desire each for the other's greatest happiness and good.

There has been also a diminishing of outside concerns so that the family can focus on its own development under its own relationship with its own Lord.

And third, there has begun to appear in the family life a community of purpose. Everybody wants the same thing, is going in the same direction, and has the same high goal.

Based on separation, devotion, and oneness of purpose and aim, most any family can make it most anywhere.

DANGEROUS FATHERS

Who Is Father?
Only the Father
The Pious Kind
The Slave Kind
The Silent Kind
The Omnipotent Kind
The Hungry Kind
Better Than You Think
For Fathers Only

Who Is Father?

IN THAT DELIGHTFUL BROADWAY PLAY "FANNY," THE SAILOR MARIUS at last returns to Marseille. Months before he had left his disappointed father, César, and his sweetheart, Fanny, to run away to sea. In Fanny's great distress she turns to Panisse, huge and bristling, powerful and tender. He marries Fanny, gives her child a name, and a father. When Marius returns, he is dumbfounded to find out what has happened. Of course he wants Fanny. Of course he wants his own child, and in a despairing moment he cries to César, "Who is the father, the one who gives life or the one who buys the bibs?" And Pinza, in the role of César, comes to his finest moment in the play when he says tenderly to Marius, *"The Father is the one who loves!"*

Most fathers would refuse any charge that they do not love; most fathers do love. But the mothers who talk to me indicate that the one thing wives and children regret and resent most in fathers is not that they are overbearing, not that they are tyrannical, not that they are selfish, not that they are authority-ridden, not that they make themselves bullies in their homes—it is not even the fact that they do not love—it is the *passivity* of their love. That is to say, they feel most fathers just do not give themselves to their wives and to their children. They are preoccupied with other things.

Sometimes she talks like this: "Oh, sure, I know Jim loves me. If it were some open enemy of my home, I would know how to face that; I could face a rival better than I can face this awful passiveness that leans on me and makes a mother out of me, lets me make all the decisions, makes me exercise all the responsibility, forces me to do all the deciding and buying and correcting."

Surely the father is the one who loves, but the father is not the one who loves passively—he is the one who loves *actively*.

I know several little boys who get most of the fathering they ever get from some old man on the block who will listen to them every day. I know several boys who have gotten most of their fatherhood from some scoutmaster who loved them actively, or from some teacher. Many a child gets its fathering from someone outside the family circle, because it is someone outside the family circle who has time, opportunity, and talent for loving them most actively.

"How can you live with a man who simply will not give himself out at all, who takes all for granted—wife and children, home and meals, and everything that goes on at home?" The answer is, "You can't!" A man who will not communicate himself to his loved ones, sooner or later becomes a fellow who *cannot* communicate; he has buried himself in his passiveness and loses all the advantages that fatherhood can give. Who is really father then? The one who actively loves. Sometimes it takes quite a bit of doing. But I tell you this can cover a multitude of other weaknesses.

What is a father anyhow? Look it up in a good, big dictionary. The word has twelve or fifteen possible meanings; is very much the same in Old German, Old Irish, Old Saxon, French, Latin, Sanskrit, and Dutch. Ten languages give almost the same root of the word in English spelled "father." Down the list half a column, about the ninth or tenth meaning, buried unless you look for it, is what appears to be etymologically the root meaning of the word "father"—"the source or prototype." That is, the father is *"that one from whom I get my strength."* Sometimes the reverse is true. The father is the one from whom my lack of strength comes.

In any kind of world we know now that the father is not the only one from whom strength comes. There is as much and more from the mother's side. We know that the father is not the only one from whom the child's weakness comes. His environment, and his teachers, and his friends have tremendous influence on both his strength and his weakness. But in the root meaning of the word the father is "the source." When Jesus used the word "father," it meant "that one from whom I get my strength." What is a father? He is the one who gives me my strength.

A serious question: What do my children need me to be as a father? And why, in heaven's name, am I made so that I am so seldom what they really need me to be?

Just as often as youngsters go outside the family for love, so often do they go outside the family to find a source of strength, the one they want to follow, the one they wish to be like. This is a great burden for the father who lives with his own children, but it's also a great encouragement for a fellow who has already the task of being father to children whom he did not sire.

Nor does the strength that comes from a father always depend on his proximity. Once I was privileged to travel many miles through the country that General Dean had wandered across on foot when he was trying to get back to the American lines at the opening of the Korean War. I spent a day in the little town of Chon-ju where he was brought in as a captive and heard there the story I later read in his book. During the second winter of General Dean's captivity one of his interrogators told the general that he had a few minutes to write a farewell note to his family. General Dean had no reason whatsoever to believe he would ever have any chance to say any other word to any member of his family, he had no way of knowing the letter would ever be delivered, but he was morally certain that in less than thirty minutes he would be taken out of his little cabin and shot. What, under those circumstances, would you write to your only son? What would be the word you would say if you were truly father?

I was fascinated by his letter. There are only eight or nine lines of it, but right in the middle of the letter General Dean said, "Tell Bill the word is *integrity*." What would you say under the same circumstances? Tell Bill the word is "popularity"? Tell Bill the word is "security"? Tell Bill the word is "happiness"? The word General Dean chose is a bigger one than they all. "Tell Bill," he said, "the word is integrity."

I think any boy would be proud to have received his strength from a father who used a word like that as the center of life's real meaning.

Who is a father? A father is the one who loves; a father is the one who gives strength. How good it is when the father can be that one who gives strength, that one who loves, as well as that one who gave life in the beginning!

Only the Father

THERE ARE, OF COURSE, THOSE WHO DECRY THE MORAL FITNESS OF modern homes. But those who have looked too long at the modern picture need to take a longer backward look. For most of us any knowledge of social conditions of two hundred years ago would come primarily from *Forever Amber* or some such type of novel. Not many of us have bothered to read Samuel Johnson, or Lecky, or the letters of Horace Walpole, or the works of Jonathan Swift, or the more serious works of Defoe. Any serious study of the primary sources of family life of two hundred years ago would reveal that the gains of modern homes over the common home of that period are almost unbelievable in scope. The gains in health, morals, humaneness, comfort, education, and religion, are unreckonable.

In the early days of the reign of Queen Anne nearly seventy-five of every one hundred babies died before they were five years of age. Queen Anne herself gave birth to seventeen children, only one of whom lived to the age of eleven. In the matter of morals, two hundred years ago the mother Parliament of all modern bodies of government had to adjourn day after day because no one was sober enough to carry on business. The ordinary street fight was marked by gouging, murder, and mayhem; and even women advertized in the papers their prowess as first-line prize fighters and defenders of their own peculiar brand of faith.

Now there are still trouble spots. Let's not be naïve about the thing. Less than ten minutes from where you are you can drive past homes of squalor and misery, homes where disorder maintains, where there is an unbelievable lack of industry and thrift and sobriety and hope and courage and humaneness. All those things are still here, but which of us could deny that the whole picture is infinitely improved. Society has said it must be so. We no longer need the laws that were needed in 1750 to keep fathers from committing their five-year-old boys to working all day in cesspools where wool was bleached in uric acids. We no longer need the laws that could hang a father for the theft of a loaf of bread. But the basic needs of children are the same.

A child of two hundred years ago needed a chance to breathe, needed a chance to live, needed something to eat. Today's crop of children are, in our society, guaranteed some sort of help and protection in the business of living. But today's children still have certain basic needs *that only the right kind of father can really supply*. This remains true in any age.

There are fundamentals that every child born into this world has an innate right to receive from its own father, if that father is alive: A child has a right to receive the necessities of life from the one who sired him. I am speaking now of the physical necessities; food, shelter, clothing. I am speaking now of spiritual necessities; the warm sense of security, the sterling example of integrity, the upthrust of a continuing devotion that a child can respect. A child has a right to those guarantees of internal security that ought to come from the one who sired him. In certain rare instances, where death or physical incapacity intervenes, the damage is not so great if the child knows that the devotion was there; but what absolutely wrecks a youngster is to feel that those who should have been able to guarantee him life's securities in his infancy just didn't want to guarantee them. There are certain fundamental guarantees I say a child deserves from his father.

There is also another basic right of the child. It is twofold really, a kind of educative process. Of course I know about our education system and believe in it. I know about our religious institutions and believe in them and participate in them. I know of our community enterprises and do all I can to support and undergird with what strength I have, but there are certain educative processes in which the father ought to share, ought to be a prime contributor. From him the child has a right to expect something. I mean *the process of transmittal of values already arrived at*—that part of education that comes from behind us. From behind us there come to each of us certain values, certain principles, certain fundamentals that the past has demonstrated to be terrifically important; and a child has a right to have transmitted to him from his father those things that have transmittal value—light from the past that belongs to us.

But there is another part of education in the home that is just as fundamental and just as important—too many children that I know have had to develop their own thirst to get something new without parental influence or guidance or support. And it seems to me that a child needs to have from his father *the push to new light, and new opportunity, and new truth*. He needs to learn from his father that his own back yard is not the world; and he needs to know from the thrust within his own father's heart and within his own father's hunger that there isn't anything like a hunger of the mind—and a child must be encouraged from infancy to have that rabid appetite to know what lies beyond his own little horizon. In that educative process in which the home centers there are only two aspects—light from the past that is worth keeping, and light that will fall on the future when youngsters are encouraged to go beyond their own bailiwick to the new horizons. What a contribution a father makes when, realizing how limited his own world is, he seeks some new world for his own children.

The Pious Kind

SOME FATHERS ARE DANGEROUS. ON ONE OF THE TELEVISION SHOWS there was a wonderful shot of a Bengal tiger and his wife and some little tigers. The commentator seemed surprised that the old man wasn't trying to eat the little fellows up, and said that was unusual for tigers. I was watching the program with my unmarried daughters and I asked the least one, "Is this true? Do tigers sometimes eat up their own babies?" And she said, "Why, yes, but didn't you know papa cats will do that sometimes, and so will papa lions, and in fact any papas in the cat family are liable to eat up their babies if they can get to them. And even sometimes daddy bears will do it, and daddy hamsters do it."

Now most of this was new to me, so I went ahead to inquire, "Why is it so that these animal papas will sometimes try to eat up their own little babies?" The concensus in the conference was that the papas are jealous. The minority report was that they aren't jealous so much as they are afraid. Maybe they are afraid that when the kids grow up they may eat up the old man. This sometimes happens in today's world. I recall having seen an old stallion work over a colt. Once I saw a bull elk half destroy a yearling that wandered up to the herd. At any rate, we know, and the point is this, that fathers are sometimes dangerous.

In the human family we know very well the spectacular kind of dangerous daddy. We know all about the driving drunks and the hot-tempered, authoritative, mean-spirited people. We read about them in the paper, and we have seen the story about some father in a fit of anger who has destroyed one of his own. However, I'm speaking of a much more respectable kind of danger; and I'm speaking of a much more respectable kind of father. I am speaking of a much more widespread danger and also of one certainly not so obvious around us.

Many of the people I see claim to have fathers who are pious, God-fearing, hard-working, respectable, orthodox, rigidly honest citizens. Yet these people have rejected all the ways of life and all the religious values their fathers claim to have. There is an interesting correlation there to me. Now certainly there are dangers from hypocrisy, and a certain kind of so-called free-thinking, and in moral irresponsibility, and that dissoluteness wherein a man just comes unglued morally, so to speak, and flies apart into all sorts of crazy activities. We know of that kind of danger. But I'm speaking of the danger that comes to us from religious fathers.

The most dangerous case is not that in which the father is a freethinker, or even a hypocrite. The danger is greater when the father is a pious, God-fearing man, when the child is inwardly and deeply convinced of it, and yet in spite of all this observes that a profound unrest is deeply hidden in his father's soul, so that not even piety and the fear of God can give him peace. The danger lies just here, that the child, in this relationship, is almost compelled to draw a conclusion about God that, after all, God is not infinite love.

A father may claim to have all that religion can give him. This is a bad mistake. If a father takes an attitude of self-piety and goodness and moral control and honesty, if he builds himself up in the eyes of his child as a rigidly perfect man of religion, he may claim all that religion can give him as his own; but if he does, he had better be certain that he is through with needs, sin, agony, frustration, doubt, or despair. For if he loses any of that supremacy in religion he claimed to have, if he transfers the authority and power of his own religious experience over into the lives of his children and tries to act like a little demigod, while the child knows that his daddy is lonely and hungry and fearful and that his faith wavers, and that there are moral gaps in his life, then what else can the youngster do but say, "What do I have to do with *his* God?" "Since my father claims to have all that religion, since he claims to be such a pious, God-fearing, sober citizen and is so rigidly moral and so completely honest, yet in his life appear these big gaps, these heartbreaking needs and agonies, these soul-splitting doubts, since he claims to have it and yet his life is as miserable as I know it must be, *what do I want with any faith like his faith.*"

Fathers are shocked at the thought that their piety can be dangerous. But the only kind of piety that's worth a fig in today's world is the kind of piety that will not close the ceiling over its own faith, the kind of faith that relaxes its rigidity and will not grow self-opinionated or uncommunicative; that will not become dour and rib-sided and closed in and unyielding, and

43

will not assume that it has the last word in everything. This kind of faith causes a man to refuse to be a demigod to his kids because he himself is still a seeker. He has not yet arrived. Therefore, tension and grief and despair, and the lapses and the gaps, and the needs that are in his life, are there simply because he admits openly and freely in communication with his children that he has not yet arrived at all faith can give him. There is an open ceiling over him, and he with his children can grow into continuing repentance and continuing communication. He has not sealed himself off in an antiseptic room that says he has arrived at all faith can give.

Pious men may see very impious results in the lives of their children. But such a man as I have described in this latter case, a pious, God-fearing man who knows he has not arrived at all faith can give him, and who has never tried to live as if he had arrived, and who will not assume this status with his children, and who lives openly with his agonies and the doubts that belong in a growing faith, is not likely to lose his way or his children. They may say that father never did make it. But they will never say he was not seeking right. They'll say, "father must have been a wonderful Christian. He was a seeker all his life, and he found a lot, but he never did think he had found it all." They will not reject the way of life on which he had started but which has not yet arrived. What kind of dangerous fathers are we anyhow when our faith can chase our children away from faith?

The Slave Kind

THE SLAVE KIND OF FATHER CAN HAPPEN ANYWHERE A MAN HAS an idea, or a calling, or a position, or his art, or a hobby, or a job, or even possessions. Do you remember that as a child you sang, "John Brown's body lies a-mouldering in the grave"? John Brown became completely obsessed with the idea of the wrongness of slavery. A huge behemoth of a man with a fiery tongue, fanatical devotion, and a good mind, he stirred up revolutions and riots for some years before he was hanged at Harper's Ferry. But all the time that he was applying such tremendous pressures against the slavery issue his wife and his thirteen children were living in absolute poverty. Ridden by illness and starvation, they existed on the little mountain farm in the Adirondacks. Nine of the children died, mostly from malnutrition and neglect. Two of the sons were killed in his wild campaigns, even though they refused to give their own heart loyalties to what John Brown was talking about. He wrote that he would never release them from their call to follow their father. In becoming immortal himself he absolutely destroyed his children. One of the last men to die in the Harper's Ferry raid was his own son whom he sent out to attempt to negotiate with those who had him surrounded. After his boy was mortally wounded in the courtyard and crawled back into the arsenal to die, the father was singularly unmoved by the destruction of his family.

This is an extreme illustration of the slavery I am talking about; but there are other kinds of slave fathers. In our time the men who are particularly prone to be dangerous fathers are salesmen, executives, preachers, lawyers, college professors, scholars—men who have become so absorbed in some limited field that they can escape anything, particularly the claims of those who are around them. Sometimes these things can wreck what would have been our highest and best part of life. Men whose high calling and gifts divert them from the needs of their family are always in danger. The slave kind I illustrated with John Brown, but there are salesmen, there are executives, there are storekeepers, there are lawyers, there are preachers, ministers, there are teachers, professors, scholars—men of most walks of life who, through their complete devotion to limited values, destroy the most precious possession.

Now you might ask why we are so prone to be dangerous fathers of the slave kind. Some want an excuse to escape the claims of family. Some want to be away from those they say they love the best. They seek a refuge. They search for escape. They find a release in their job, in their calling, in their ideas, in their work, in their study. Others are absolutely innocent in it, caught in it. Committed to doing a job too big for us, we drive ourselves to do it and innocently pay far too high a price for such a way of life. There are others who secretly enough, unknown to themselves certainly, are punishing themselves, even destroying themselves, in the act of subconsciously destroying the ones they love the most. Certainly it ought to be obvious that for many of us success—the driving urge to win on through —is a more than normal expression of aggression. Now of course there are hates in every human life, just as there ought to be loves in every human life, but it's a tragic, tragic thing when that subconscious hate and aggression expresses itself against a family.

Now you have a right to ask a question something like this: What's this guy trying to do, persuade all of us who have high callings, professions, community standing and responsibility, to turn into a bunch of homebodies and do nothing but wait on the kids? Well, it might have its advantages, considering how many of your wives are still working ten, twelve, fourteen years after your marriage. Somebody ought to turn into a housewife in many of the houses I know, but that's not my point at all. I am trying to face for myself and with you a problem any man faces whose work takes him away too much from those he really loves the most. If you find yourself using your job as an excuse to be away from your family, ask yourself what is wrong. What is really wrong that makes you want to be away from your family?

If your work honestly pulls you away, that is to say, if, no beating around the bush about it, your work just requires your absence from your family far too much, ask yourself two questions: Is it worth it? Do I have to do this?

A special friend of mine had been on the road for many, many years. He was fed up with it. For years he had liked old furniture, and now I believe he is one of the happiest men I know because he has opened a secondhand furniture place and is doing a thing he loves, and doing well with what he has, and has made for himself a really new home life that he had missed for the years when his work took him away. He resolved his question by saying, "No, it really wasn't worth it to be away so much!"

But suppose it is worth it. Suppose, to you, your work is worth being away. Then, there are two things I could suggest. Plan to relieve the tensions of neglect as regularly as a week end comes around or as your time at home comes around. Plan to relieve the long periods of isolation by daily communication —by telephone, special messages; gifts won't always substitute but they are something. You plan to relieve the tensions of neglect that your high calling imposes on you and your family. You learn to give yourself to what I call "island living." Perhaps it would be more clearly expressed if I say bring as little of your job home with you as you possibly can. It ought to be an island for you; and if, as with myself, a lot of your work has to be done at home, then learn to welcome the interruptions that come anywhere there are children, anywhere there are pets, anywhere there's a house. If you've got a house, live in all of it, especially if you have to work in it. There are ways that we can overcome these separations and still achieve both a rank in that high calling and a position in the hearts of that dearest group on earth—our family.

The Silent Kind

FOR WANT OF A BETTER NAME, CALL HIM "THE SILENT KIND," AND he is a very dangerous father. There is a wide range for this kind of dangerous father. It goes all the way from the strong Western hero on the one hand, to the sick, uncommunicative John P. Milquetoast on the other hand. Strangely enough, faulty communication—between fathers and mothers, and father and children—is one of the two or three big marital problems. I am not altogether sure what causes it—some men are the silent type because of a fear of objectivity, the fear of anything outside themselves. Others give you the silent treatment because of their preoccupation with other things. They really are absorbed, and they never seem to be able to focus on the values and the situation immediately at hand. Some become victims of this habit of uncommunicativeness simply through laziness and selfishness. It is easier to settle within one's self, and for people who particularly like themselves it is sometimes much more pleasant. Others become uncommunicative because of immaturity, childlikeness —but the most obvious are those who use that withdrawn, silent, hide-in-the-corner way of living as an attention-getter. We can just get more attention from our children if we seem hurt or hangdog, or pull away from the center of things. People really focus their attention on one who will not communicate. Any time anything comes up that is the least bit controversial, papa goes silent. He clams up, he freezes, he goes within himself; and it is an expression of disagreement, abuse, hostility, and resentment all in one. It always amazes me how talkative some of these silent fellows get when they are away from their families. They are positively garrulous; they really become the center of things; they really communicate!

How many families there are where the mother must be both father and mother simply because the father will not pay the price of communication! He communicates everywhere else, but at home he gives you the old silent treatment. He will go around for days with his mouth all turned down and his eyes all turned in. You get the impression that something fatal has come up and he is just determined to wait it out; he will just sit and see what is going to happen.

This grows, and the first thing you know the family has planned some big get-together with lots of company in, some very special occasion, and papa is absent. The most powerful weapon he can have at his disposal is just not to be there. So he doesn't show. This is a form of desertion. It is a kind of surrender. It is almost the same as moving away, for a father to refuse to communicate himself to his wife and his children.

There are five or six forms this kind of desertion may take: *overdependence*—mother even fixes his ties for him, though I will admit that might improve the situation sometimes; it expresses itself by a kind of *inattentiveness*—he just doesn't know what is going on in the lives of the children, and though he may care, he simply can't show any interest; a kind of *helplesssness* —he will stand in front of a problem for four or five days, unable to decide which way to go. In some cases this desertion appears as a kind of *overmeekness,* and in others as a rank *indifference;* and of course the ultimate form of it is *desertion*. But the base of the whole thing is that this man has just simply refused to give himself to any other, and particularly to those to whom he ought to be close. This is dangerous and is the very essence of irreligion. It is the essence of self-ness. It is what we mean in religion when we say a fellow is lost. He doesn't know how to communicate—not only with God, but with those on earth dearest and nearest to him.

There is no hope for a man who cannot enter into any kind of communion, for religion is the essence of communion, and the family is the essence of religious relationships. There is no family possible where there is no real communion. This is also the essence of despair that Sören Kierkegaard talks about in two of his works. Kierkegaard says the essence of despair is to be unwilling to be the self before the self. It is the meaning of despair, but it is also the meaning of the sorriest kind of religion known, self-love or self-hate. If at your house father has gone into that dangerous kind of living that will not commune with those he loves the best, sometimes with patience and warmth and love and understanding he can be led out of it. I hope he can still want to be free of it before it is everlastingly too late. And it gets too late in more families than I can name.

The Omnipotent Kind

I WANT TO TALK ABOUT THE ALL-SUFFICIENT GUY WHO CAN HANDLE anything his children ever need him to handle. This smart fixer, this keen manipulator, this man-about-town, this fellow who knows his way around—he can become a very dangerous kind of father. He can so construct an image of himself in the minds and lives and hearts of his children that they actually grow up with the notion that daddy can handle anything.

All children think this at first; but they deserve to learn better from their own father. I remember very keenly that I felt this way about my own father. One day a young neighbor of mine, now a fine surgeon, broke his Daisy air rifle—I was quite confident my father could fix anything. So I took the gun home for my omnipotent earthly father to fix. I never shall forget the chagrin with which a little boy learned from his father that his father was a very human being and that some things are beyond repair. Some children of some fathers never really learn this. They grow up thinking their daddy owns the earth. He may be out of his depth most of his life, and they find it out in such a shocking way and lose the father they really would have needed in their early adult years.

It is a dangerous kind of father who lets his children think he can answer all life's problems; who never uses the words "I don't know"; who never runs out of ability to help or decide; who never permits his children to develop within themselves the ability to face problems. He denies his children the knowledge that he himself, as father, needs to depend upon someone beyond himself. Actually this is a bad kind of ego manifestation. But perhaps you can get the notion from a story.

Three or four years ago now, I was boarding a plane in a western city, and someone tapped me on the shoulder; I turned around to recognize a man whom I had known when he was a lad and I was a very young pastor. We got on the plane together and entertained ourselves all the way to San Francisco by swapping stories about his home. Somewhere during that rather nostalgic conversation I mentioned the name of the little girl he used to run around with, thinking that he had married her. He said, "No, I didn't marry Betsy. I married a girl I met over at the university." And so my next question was,

"Well, what happened to Betsy?" "Oh," he said, "didn't you know? Joe got her, but let me tell you how I got over it."

Now, my friend was one of four brothers—orphans—and when school was out they worked in their uncle's market until dark or closing time. They worked hard; they learned early the meaning of a dollar; they learned how to save; they learned how to be reliable; they learned how to keep accounts; they learned how to wait on people and how to deal with the public. "Nearly every afternoon," he said, "during my junior year in high school, Joe would ride by in front of the market with my girl friend in a bright blue, shiny Buick. I just ate my heart out for weeks, for that fellow was beating my time and there wasn't anything I could do about it. But my uncle was a wiser man than I thought. He caught me once standing there half blubbering because I had lost my girl to this city slicker, so to speak, and he came and got me by the arm and led me back to his little private office. He got down on one knee in front of an old iron safe and twisted some knobs and opened it up; out of a little tin box he lifted a piece of paper that I recognized as a note; the face of it was $1,000 and it was signed by Joe's daddy. It was a note for $1,000 worth of unpaid groceries that he owed my uncle while his son was driving around in an automobile he couldn't afford, stealing my girl. Somehow I got a great relief out of that thing." Then my friend added: "I also learned something—that that fellow who had seemed to be to his children and to our whole town such a real big-shot really wasn't so omnipotent at all. Since then I've never grieved for a moment over any false values."

There comes a time, I say, for all earthly fathers when they come to the limit of their capacity; indeed, one of the most subtle temptations of modern life is for a father to try to be everything to his children, to try to give everything to his children, and procure anything for them. I think children need to know from fathers that there is a limit to what they can expect, that there is a limit to what the father can give, there is an edge to what he can know, there is an end to his own strength. I say it is better if they learn this from him. It is extremely hard if they have to learn it because of the collapse of a father, or a father's reputation—a father who has stretched himself too far in his attempt to be omnipotent.

For, you see, there comes a time when your father must become a very human being. It happens to everybody's daddy. I say there comes a time when your father must become a very human being—subject to illness, disease, weakness, old age, despair, fatigue, ignorance, prejudice, bad judgment, poor vision —just like all the rest. For his sake and for yours, I hope he has not pretended to a power that he doesn't have as a human being. And for your sake, I hope when you have discovered that your father is a very human being, that you can also learn that you are very human too.

The Hungry Kind

THE HUNGRY KIND OF FATHER IS THE IMMATURE FATHER, AND HE is dangerous. Let me show you some varied symptoms, in order to show you a single dangerous disease—immaturity.

Let's say, for example, that out at your house there's a father whom nothing ever pleases. He's what we call hypercritical. He doesn't like the way the children are reared; he doesn't like the way the house is kept; he doesn't like the way the food is prepared; he is even critical of himself. This is a symptom of immaturity.

On the other hand, he may be completely unreliable. He may

go so far the other way that he just doesn't seem to have any opinion about things. When the family is planning a great occasion he may be there—he may not. When there are guests coming in, he may show, or he may call thirty minutes late, or he may not think of the thing until it's over. He is almost completely unreliable and unpredictable. This is a symptom of immaturity.

Sometimes we see a father who knows all the answers, and nothing ever stumps him. He has a precise formula for any kind of problem. Everything fits into his consecutive little concentric circles of attitudes and ideas and responsibilities and law. He *is* the law, but this is immaturity.

On the other hand, he may not be dogmatic; he may go so far that he is completely defensive. He is always explaining himself, defending himself. He is usually hurt about something. He has always the business of making himself look good in the eyes of his wife, his children, his neighbors, or his co-workers, or his superiors. There's a deep, ingrained fear somewhere, and he's always afraid that he won't quite measure up. This again is immaturity.

Frequently the immature kind of father may be very penurious. He doles what he makes out in little dabs—little driblets. He may have to, I grant you that. But at the same time he exercises a rigidity of control that does not share any of the responsibility. Or another extreme, he may be completely irresponsible. He welcomes the wife's desire to have something to say about the family budget, and he seems to get a great satisfaction out of bringing home everything that he makes and putting it at her disposal. Then through the rest of the week he gets a great deal of satisfaction out of wheedling what can be gotten from her for extra little things.

Now the strange thing about all these fathers is that they may be all six of these: hypercritical and unreliable, dogmatic and defensive, penurious and irresponsible. But whether he's one or two, or all six of them, the disease is ordinarily one and the same. It's *the disease of immaturity*. The father bids for attention. He wants to be the center of things. He's the hungry kind.

Sometimes I talk to a wife who describes the problems that are almost wrecking her home or her marriage; sometimes children drop by to talk about such things. Without any accusations at all I'll sometimes say, "Are you trying to tell me he is really a little boy?" And a face will light up and say, "Why, yes, that's what I mean, he's just like a little boy next door." And actually he is. Sometimes he grows up and becomes more like an adolescent, but really the adolescent kind of immaturity is harder to live with and to handle than the little-boy kind. At any rate, whether he's hypercritical or unreliable, whether he's dogmatic or defensive, whether he is irresponsible or penurious with the family income, he is immature.

More than frequently such a father comes from a broken home, or an immature home—an environment of emotional instability. And usually, not always, but usually, there are bad connections between this father and his own mother and his own father. Unfilled he is. He has never been filled up. He was neither properly weaned nor properly nourished. He is unfilled, and he is still seeking fulfillment. He's unfilled, and he still wants to get instead of give. He has never learned adult giving. He is unfilled, and therefore he is in a chronic and constant competition with his own children for their mother's attention. Actually, in many ways he is just another child. Unable to accept himself as he is, he won't let you accept him.

Frequently he finds a substitute for that unfilledness, a substitute for something he didn't have in boyhood; sometimes it's a substitute for something he is failing to find in his own home relationship. With some men it has become alcohol. There is quite a connection between the two kinds of bottle. Sometimes the substitute becomes gambling, a feverish thing that gnaws at a man. Sometimes it's extramarital relationships with all the agonies and griefs they can cause. Sometimes it goes to the other extreme and is a kind of puritanism, rigid and cold and withdrawn. Sometimes the substitute that fills his hunger is an excess emotionalism in religion, for an immature man can be devoutly religious. Sometimes it's food—a man becomes one of those people who literally cram to try to get some sort of emotional relief. Sometimes it's an interference and a competition with the children. At any rate, whether it's a hypercriticism or an unreliability, whether it's a dogmatism or a defensiveness, whether it's a penuriousness or an irresponsibleness, the disease back of it all is immaturity.

What about a remedy? Why, the most witless thing imaginable would be for me to propose a stock answer! There isn't any unless some of my divine-healer friends could take a crack at this. They could really do us some good if they could handle the problem of immaturity in marriage. Yet there is a step taken in the right direction toward a more mature home when you recognize that the problem is there. The problem is not just hypercriticism or nagging or irresponsibility or hurt feelings. The problem is deeper. And when you recognize that it's there, you've made a step in the right direction.

It helps to know what you're dealing with. Here you're not dealing with just an emotional thing—you're dealing with a deep unfilledness on the inside. It can be recognized by its victims and faced, which is the first step toward recovery. You—the wife, the children, the family—you can accept the reality of his needs. They are very real needs and with love and sympathy you can go to meet them. You can provide part of an answer and you are the only one who can provide this part of the answer, because he is attached to you. He is yours. Help him, then, by understanding what it is that drives him into these expressions of immaturity.

Better Than You Think

MOST SONS HAVE IT BETTER THAN THEIR FATHERS HAD IT. WITH better education, better income, better job, we live in more expensive houses and certainly have more gadgets. Whether or not we live in better homes is still an open question. But most sons have it better than their fathers had it.

Because most sons know they have got it better than their fathers had it, many make a crudely, crassly false assumption about their own worth compared to that of the old man. And there is rather widespread rejection on the part of these blasé and successful young men of the values of previous generations. Some I know are ashamed that the old man doesn't make a better appearance. Some are embarrassed that their father didn't finish grammar school—he went to work. Some are chagrined that his vocabulary doesn't show any more worldly wisdom, and others are disappointed because their father really didn't amount to more.

Now any father any age learns early that he must not expect too much special attention, too much special favor, too much special concern. He learns, if he is a real father, that most of his life he has to give and not worry too much about getting. Even though he had secret hopes that maybe everybody would throw in together and get him a gun, he grins when it turns out to be a tie. And though he wanted that nice new pipe he saw in the window, he is pleased with a handkerchief—and the new outboard motor never does show up, but a shirt comes in occasionally, and he lives with it, because he learns that the family puts a different evaluation on his value. But regardless, there are one or two things that he is entitled to have from you, even though you have it a great deal better than he had it. Before I come to that, let me ask you, What kind of man is your father really?

Is he still on the same job, or if not on the same job, is he still engaged in the same craft, or has he maintained the same professional connection over a period of years? Has he been able to build himself into a real relationship with the same firm?—Has he stayed put? If he has, the likelihood is that he is a man of stability, of character, of skill. Is your father a man who is conscious of his obligations? And as long as you have known him, has he met his obligations like an honest man? Is your father a man who has respect for what is right? Whether it goes against him or not, is he a fellow whom you really believe to have a regard for the right or the wrong of things? Did he want you to live in a larger circle than he had, whether he could give it to you or not? That is to say, did he know that there was a bigger world than his own?

If you can say he is a kind man—that is, one who can give himself to a family—if he has been able to show that he loves children, if he loves the one whom he married; and if, in addition, you feel that your father is a devout man, that he has found some eternal values in worship and in faith, beyond what we measure and count, then he is worthy of more than your respect—he is worthy of your *emulation; you ought not to mark him off*. You ought not to assume, because you have a better job and a better house and went to school longer, that you are worth more. Maybe he did better than you think.

Some of us need to re-evaluate by what process and by what sacrifice our parents determined, when we were little children, that our world would have a wider horizon than their world had had. I can recall my parents deciding to make a gift from the pay check to a certain institution that had lost its administration building by fire because they had a hope that someday their children would have a chance to attend such a school. Even if your father can't read a menu and doesn't know the difference between "frappé" and "filet," if he splits his infinitives and eats with his knife, and says archaic words when he asks the blessing, the chances are he did better with the tools he had at his disposal than we are doing with the magnificent tools at our disposal.

So it is, as a fellow comes into more mature years of young manhood, he begins to appreciate and understand something of the cost, sacrifice, character, energy, drive, love, involved in the fatherhood of those in the generation just before us who have given us these open doors. We begin to gain a new respect for integrity, steadiness, righteousness, freedom from one's own limited circle, kindness, devoutness, and we look with a new and healthier respect across and up to the men who make us or have made us what we are. Sometimes we have to learn it the hard way, as did Elijah under his juniper tree, crying, "Alas, I am no better than my fathers." None of us really is. Man is advancing everywhere, we say, but Goethe reminds us: "Man remains always the same!"

As a man gets older he is less and less impressed with the external march of things, the so-called progress of civilization, and he comes to realize that his needs and his longings, his emptiness and his cravings, are those that his fathers and his grandfathers knew; and he comes to feel himself more and more at one with their needs and longings and desires; and, perhaps, he comes at last to understand that they had some tremendously valid insights and he is grateful for the kingdom of love with which they sometimes surrounded him.

And perhaps I can entertain the hope that this will catch the fancy of some man who has made the mistake of assuming, on the basis of mere and shallow surface trappings, that he had something his father didn't have. Maybe if the old man could pay his debts, and could trust, and could love, he was bigger than you thought.

For Fathers Only

DAGWOOD SOMETIMES REMINDS US THAT "HUSBANDS ARE A SORRY lot." By and large, this is in our minds about fathers in general, but if it is so, we certainly do not mean to be. It is mainly that we start off under such an awful handicap. I know no books on the prenatal care of fathers. And even though it is reported that Eskimo fathers go through the pangs of birth in sympathy with their wives, still, by and large, having the baby is the mother's business.

That is to say, most fathers begin their fatherhood as nothing more than a *biological incidental*. The baby is born in a hospital; the father is not in the room; he knows nothing of the last stages of labor; he not only can't touch the child in the hospital, he can't even be in his wife's room when it is brought in to nurse, but he is forced to stand outside in the hall and stare through plate glass at that little red and squalling collection of protoplasm that they say is his. He didn't have it, and he can't hold it. He can only try to pay for it—which means to say that pretty soon he graduates.

He is no longer a biological incidental, he becomes an *economic necessity*. He pays the hospital bill, if he can, and brings the mother and baby home. There he is met by an expert in the form of his mother-in-law who qualifies as an expert because she had a baby twenty years ago, and is, therefore, in complete charge. At no time is a young mother more completely dependent upon her own mother than in the first hours of trying to learn to take care of the new baby. About all the father gets to do is to wash out a few diapers—at which he is awfully inept—and he usually leaves enough soap in the rinse water to irritate the child thoroughly before it is three days old. Gingerly he holds it, but it was tied to him by no umbilical cord. The only pangs he suffered at birth were the pangs of anxiety, and it's almost impossible for him to become more than a biological incidental and an economic necessity.

The situation is further complicated with thousands of youngsters in the present generation because the father was away in military service for a period of three to five years, and the five to ten years since haven't helped too much. The youngster had a great head start on the father before he ever became part and parcel of the young fellow's life.

Then comes adolescence. The youngster is at least three-fourths grown. He becomes a strange, wild, irrepressible creature. He is flunking his geometry, running around with the wrong gang, and, because he is using all his energy to grow up, seems to be mighty lazy. Sooner or later he gets into some kind of minor trouble. And then almost before the father knows it he has moved from biological incidental through economic necessity to *responsible party*. And he is bewildered by it all. He is not quite sure how he got to be the responsible party or how he can carry out the responsibility that has almost suddenly become his.

It's a tough spot to be in. Maybe you will forgive me if I sound like a responsible party for a few minutes and try to give some practical suggestions for fathers who are caught in this predicament. They are simple and I believe easy to follow.

Fathers ought to be accessible—available. Much of my own work is done in my study at home. It is work that is done at its best under conditions of quiet and isolation. In addition, my work requires hours out away from home—sometimes very long hours. I resolved that there would never be a lock on the door where I am doing my work during hours at home. I have a hunch that many a sermon has been a little bit better because there was a grimy handprint on some of my notes. I know many a long, dull, flat place has been lifted to an elevated height by an intrusion from one of the younger members of my family, or from one of the ten or twelve grand youngsters that run in and through my study in company with my own. Fathers ought to be available, even if it means running the risk of stepping, sock-footed, on a set of "jacks" left in the middle of the study floor.

Everyone in the family ought to know that daddy is interested in everything that interests any member of the family. Now this may well mean that you will listen to your six-year-old read one of her little books as she sits on the clothes hamper in the bathroom while you are shaving in the morning. But, even so, she ought to know that you are mighty interested to know how well she has developed.

Under every circumstance, even the most stressful, fathers ought to be kind. I find it so difficult not to impose my own inner frustrations on those who are under my care. Frankly, it is sometimes hard to learn to be kind. Children deserve to remember a father who was always kind.

Fathers must practice the business of letting the day slip off behind them as they come in the front door, or the back, whichever it happens to be at their house. Fathers should never assume that physical care and economic security are all his family really wants from him. Every family I know hungers for more than that from its father. Even if they are brilliant attorneys or learned professors, fathers ought to include themselves in family play. A game of Old Maid, or Authors, or Chinese Checkers, or some other such "nonsense" may be far beneath their professional dignity, but there are few things more vital than family play.

Fathers must learn to think again on many levels. You have to remember how a nine-year-old looked at it. Sometimes it requires quite a trick to be able to do it. Children should be "in on" the father's family financial worries—but as a wholesome joint problem, not as a shame-bringing, worrisome sensitiveness. Perhaps this could best be handled in the family council to which I have referred. Fathers ought to know about the child's development in school, in morals, and in sexual, physical, and personality growth. But a father's interest in his child must be felt as love and companionship, not as meddlesomeness.

Fathers should remember how sensitive children are to his appearance before their friends; his attitudes, his prohibitions, his standing. Money is not too important; they simply want to be proud of him.

Fathers ought not to make mothers responsible for the religious development of the family. They ought to come all the way themselves. There are matters that must not be left to the schoolteacher, preacher, Sunday-school teacher, and scoutmaster. The child has a right to know of his father's concern in his own religious development. All children should have had at some time or another the privilege of hearing their father pray.

And maybe, someday, there will be books to help us fathers on our journey from biological incidental to real fatherhood.

MOTHERS AND SONS

Son Stay Small
Turn Him Loose
Mother or Smother
For Pete's Sake
The Mature Son
Mamma's Worst Baby
When Son Takes a Wife
Mother's Day

Son Stay Small

OF COURE THIS IS A FOOLISH VENTURE. I KNOW THAT. A MAN JUST can't talk about mothers and get away with it. Least of all can he expect to talk to mothers about their sons, and stay whole. It just isn't done! But somebody needs to, hide or no hide. The case histories of hundreds of thousands of emotionally immature sons in World War II attest that somebody ought to talk to mothers.

Men are less important to their children than women. So few fathers grow from "biological incidental" through "economic necessity" to "responsible partner" in child rearing that they really are less closely related to the parent problem. Consequently, more problem parents are mothers, even though many times mother is a problem because papa is no real father.

And to whom is mother a problem? To her little son, of course, most of all. He starts off with her, caught in a contradiction. Like this:

The first major decision a baby makes is, as Dr. Smith Ely Jelliffe says, "whether to holler or to swaller." It's a cinch he can't do both—not without breaking something. All his first years he spends a great deal of time doing one or the other. Usually, under pressure from "that woman," he "hollers," then "swallers" whatever it is she hands him.

He is four years old and "king of the cowboys." Just a minute ago he shot seven deadly gunmen and there was blood and smoke all over the place. His horse is run to exhaustion and stands piteously blowing while this grand, selfless, dashing hero stalks the last four killers on foot, with only a rubber knife and his undying courage for protection. Then shatteringly, rudely, overwhelmingly, the "hero" collapses in squalling tears as "that woman" lifts him out of his mad conflict into another conflict just as mad but more real. He hollers—but then he swallers—

his orange juice, his cod-liver oil, his bath, and indignity of indignities, his *nap*. He, a grown proud hero, must submit to this! And conflict, even hatred, at little-boy levels, springs up. He hollers bad things and mamma cries over her vicious little darling. He dreams—of *revenge,* and even sings about it in his bath tub.

Such a four-year-old is a special friend of mine. His mother, a gracious and charming young lady, horrified at his "hollering and swallering," his threats, his resentments, and his rebellion that keep her traveling faster than any mortal ought to have to go, carried him over to a psychiatrist for analysis. She was just certain no little man ought to be that hard to handle. Later, with a delightfully candid confessional smile, she told us what the psychiatrist said: "Young lady, take this perfectly normal, and very well-made young man home . . . and get hold of yourself!"

Every normal mother wants her son to be a "real boy," a "big man." She wants him to be courageous, self-confident, and able. She wants him to be the picture of virile manhood. But, as Karl Menninger puts it, she is caught in vague and variable contradictions:

If he develops so much self-assurance that he becomes self-assertive and defies her, she is scandalized and beats the daylights out of him or cries about it at night.

If he develops so much courage that he gets competitive and goes in for football, boxing, or mountain-climbing, she is frightened and hauls him back behind the screen of her protectiveness, or else becomes feverish with visions of imagined injuries.

If he develops an interest in little girls and comes to the point of normal curiosity about the differences, she is terrified by the threat of a rival and wraps around him the constricting folds of Victorian prudishness and ignorance that not even adulthood will leave behind.

Do you see it? Mother is caught in a contradiction. She wants him to grow up, but she does not want him to grow up. Disciplined by her own rearing, and by society, she is always forbidding his growth in exactly the direction that all his instincts force him to go. Even though in principle she is all for his development, she nevertheless forbids it, without knowing that her own fears, neuroses, anxieties, and timidities are being transferred in a deadly way.

This is grand larceny. This is the robber-hood of mother-hood. This is the area where the robber-mother works. Stolen: a man. Son, stay small; don't ever leave me. Son, don't grow—and mother becomes a thief.

How? By being more loyal to the patterns of her society than to the principles of human development, by transferring the restricting fears of her own rearing, she begins to *smother*. She develops an anxious concern that makes her pry into every detail of his life with a "mother-knows-all" kind of virtue to excuse her curious snooping. She robs him of all individuality and natural expressiveness in his attempts to discover his own independence; then covers up under the name of pious mothering instinct. She rebukes his early exploration of his dawning manhood and sexuality under the ban of "niceness" and "gentlemanliness" that more often is ignorant and dark with secret mysteries.

Results? A robbery! Son stay small! And all unwittingly, he has been robbed of his most precious potential—masculinity.

Then comes adolescence with its high narrow bridge to maturity. And one of three things happens: Resenting the threatened emasculation that will deny his male potential—*he breaks out*—in an overt rebellion. He asserts his maleness in some petty vandalism, abuse, troublemaking, or delinquency. He breaks windshields, he deliberately disobeys, he's a "hard-to-handle" toughie. Or, he represses his hatreds and resentments. They reappear as hatred of the "female," and he makes a sorry husband for any woman foolish enough to marry him. Or, he surrenders to this loss of individuality and never breaks out. He is tied to you long after you are dead, with a cord that no future attachment can break. Pathetic, listless, sexless, futureless, he has "stayed small." He's a good son. He never did leave you and he never will.

An old Yiddish proverb says, "God could not be everywhere, so he made mothers." I have met sons in whose behalf I could have wished that when God made some mothers, he had given them more sense.

Turn Him Loose

WITH SOMETHING OF FEAR AND TREMBLING, AND QUITE CONSCIOUS OF my own temerity, I once gave this material on mothers and sons as a television series. To my very real and surprised gratification it was received, in the main, by a gracious withholding of judgment against me, and even, here and there, with modified confession on the part of the sincere seekers after wisdom in the rearing of sons.

But one mother really spilled over. It was just too much. So I got it (anonymously and vicariously) in the neck, just where it was deserved! *She* was an intelligent mother; *she* never endured anything like it; *she* had never robbed her son; *she* wanted my wife to tell me for her (anonymously) that every time *she* turned her son loose to make any decision he got in trouble or made the wrong turn and had to run to her. He was a most belligerent adolescent in spite of *all she* had done to help him; and, besides that, *he* just sat there and grinned delightedly all through my telecast. Furthermore, she wanted me to know that since I have no sons, I had no right to speak!

Lady, I got your message—word for word! And it's true; I have no sons; all my sons are daughters; I have no right to speak. Not because I have no sons, but rather because I have never been a mother, I really have no right to speak.

However, I *am* a son and have had a mother all my life—a grand one, and smarter than either of us knew. She knew how to turn us loose and thrust us to freedom and opportunity. She, somehow, by God's grace, knew instinctively what happens to little boys kept tied too long. I salute her, not for loving me, but for loving me in a way to release both of us from the natural selfishness of mother love.

I not only am a son, I know *your* sons. On fifty college campuses, at a dozen air force bases, on several army posts, at a navy school or two, I know your sons. I have taught them briefly, at CCC camps and at high-school, college, and seminary levels. I have known them in three or four jails, before the grand jury, in the work of several churches, and in scouting—all the way from six on patrol to fifty thousand camped together at Jamboree. I know your sons.

I know some mothers too—neurotic, afraid, bewildered—and, again, many, many more who are serene, confident, able. Because I know your son and you I can tell in five minutes what you have done to him, good or bad, and it gives me right to speak.

Even so, I have no right to condemn, and would not if I could; there's too much at stake here. Out of sympathetic concern for all involved I keep remembering those fine youngsters

71

who have said to me, "How can I get my mother's hands off me?"

Now mother love is female love, demanding, possessive, retentive. How shall she turn him loose?

Certainly not as many have—out of a sense of relief or despair, or out of ignorance, or indifference, or frustration. And not, I hope, in that most painful way of all, when he is torn away from her by the army, or the authorities, or a wife.

Certainly she shall not turn him loose to find for himself his own moral level or behavior standards.

The release a mother owes her son is emotional, psychological, personal. The release she must give him is the right to manhood —and she must prepare him for it! Only in the womb is he completely hers: the rest of life is a process of separation. Indeed this is just what physical birth and its severed cord symbolize. This is the *meaning* of birth—one soul cannot be kept within another! And indeed, this is why birth is so difficult a process! Growing up is so much a matter of separation—physically, psychologically, emotionally—that some births are *never* completed, and both mother and son are in labor all their lives. How tragic, and how utterly difficult, is the life of the half-born son! And how can he be born again who has not yet been born the first time?

All of a mother's life with her son is within this process of separation begun at birth. But to say "turn him loose" is not to say "be unconcerned"! There are two things he *must* have from you—that you give him first of all:

Security-sense comes from the long, uninterrupted period of psychological mothering. This is the time of suckling and snuggling, the easy creation of habits not begun too soon out of false pride, the sense of family, the development of morals, the birth of beliefs, the sense of the presence of God. These are the years when he becomes not just son—he can't help that—but also friend of yours—and you can't bribe that. It's given and deserved, or it's lost.

Self-confidence is created by that gradual process of release to himself and to other helpers. You are concerned for where he is going, you fear he will fall, yet you let him go. You push him out. You let him ride off alone. Then maybe you sit down and write, as one mother did, about how much you owe to teachers and scouters and the rough little boys who have helped you rear your own to an undamageable self-confidence.

Give us a whole town full of boys—by giving the world your own boy. Let him be suckled in love, steadied by the long mothering months of security that can come only from you, his self-confidence not shattered by being shamed over his early bathroom habits, or hindered by your unreasonable reproaches and embarrassing remonstrances before his mates. Let him be allowed to learn at a normal rate about diet and dirt, baths, friends, girls, the questions he can't answer, the walls he can't see over, and God. Let him be trusted at home to do some things that keep stretching him; released to good teachers, rough playmates, the out-of-doors, books, girls, sports, work, and worship; encouraged in scouting, Y.M.C.A., 4-H clubs, to be away from his mother; to work, to trade, to plan, to dream—until, at seventeen—an Eagle, with his *own* wings—you can afford to let him fly alone. And you can sleep at night while he's doing it. He has wings.

Mother or Smother

BECAUSE I HAVE BEEN DEALING WITH MOTHERS AND SONS DOES NOT mean the subject of fathers has been finished. In fact, the father is frequently the *cause* of unbalanced mother-son relationships. Sometimes the father *is* the mom. More often, he keeps the fine but immature young thing he married from ever growing up and forces her into a smother relationship with her children. All this raises the question, "What makes a mother smother?"

It is especially easy for mother relations to become smother relations when the husband is not really husband. When there exists a lack, an unbalance, a failure, a lack of mutuality at any level of marriage, the woman easily gives evidence of her instability, or insecurity, by her inordinate concern for and domination of her children. This is particularly true when the physical relationships of husband and wife are not right. What really belongs to the husband-wife association is repressed, turned around, and changed—even perverted—until it forces its way into expression as so-called mother love, better call wife frustration. Again, and just as frequently, the mother's concern for her children becomes complete preoccupation when the father is not really father—for there is a father-child responsibility too. Sensing the lack of support, shared authority, responsibility, and concern in her children's father, the mother, unconsciously or consciously, gradually tries to become both father and mother. The effect is usually smothering.

Second, as a factor in making smotherers out of mothers, many place the social image, the ideal, our way of life has idolized and made mandatory for its mothers. We go overboard in the maudlin expression of inane sentiment no real mother will tolerate. Mother's Day becomes a nationwide emotional debauch with flowers, lingerie, and candy strewn everywhere in place of the true spiritual reverence motherhood deserves. Even in churches, for a day at least, men forego the worship of God for the worship of the idealized composite of mother, and there are plenty of texts for all kinds of deathless prose-sermons, telegrams, mottoes, and other inanities, Dead Thackeray is brought alive again to say, "Mother is the name of God in the lips and hearts of children." Or, if we need something really ancient, we go back to old Aristotle who may or may not have really said, "Mothers are fonder of their children than fathers; they remember the pain of bringing them forth." Even political candidates, or, one might say, especially political candidates, know how to ring the changes on the old aria of idolized, idealized motherdom. Our whole way of life joins in the chorus, creating an almost universal drift toward mother domination. The image clings, grows softer and more beautiful with time and distance, and becomes so potent a factor in our lives that honest, self-disciplined, confident mothers seem positively unconcerned along-side the rank and file who knock themselves out keeping their sons from growing up. I believe it is Karl Menninger who notes that this pressure is particularly heavy on sons in wartime. He goes on to remark that the number-one request for songs on Bing Crosby's tour of the Southwest Pacific theater during the war was for Brahm's "Lullaby."

The third cause of smother-mothers, perhaps first in importance, is plain immaturity. Edward A. Strecker, in *Their Mother's Sons,* gives page after page to a discussion of this cause of smothering. Immaturity begets immaturity. We transfer our parents' weaknesses to the rearing of our own children. Sometimes it is a revenge on those who reared us; more often it is just immaturity. Immaturity also produces shallow levels of concern. The mother becomes so completely concerned over the child's eating, washing, and bathrooming, all of which must be done precisely in order, that she never sees what she does to personality, independence, pride, and future by her emphasis on purely mechanical functions. Frequently she follows a fad that worships vitamins, thereby enriching the spinach-canners, and never really lifts her eyes for the long look. Wet diapers on a three-year-old or a sweet tooth in the baby's eating habits are such

75

major faults to be overcome that no thought is given to the long-range effect of her spiritual neglect during the most vital months of young life. Horace Bushnell was a hundred years ahead of his times when he claimed that indulgence of suckling children may make dependent alcoholics of adults. Immature preoccupation with mechanics not only makes nervous wrecks of mothers, it also makes stripped characters out of little children who are thus taught mechanical and functional values that never grow into the spiritual values essential to real adulthood.

Given an immature woman whose husband is not fully husband and father, and who lives in a world that idealizes a false picture of motherhood, you will all but invariably get smothering instead of mothering. And it's a crime.

All along some very brave men have cautioned against this. Havelock Ellis was interested. The almost smothered Augustine lashed out at his own fastenings when he cried, "Give me other mothers and I will give you another world." Hippel speaks of the crimes of smothering when he claims: "Of ten wounds a child receives, nine are from its mother." Forel wrote candidly to say that mother love is sometimes pernicious, and injures through creating illusions that never mature. Karl Menninger even makes a list of the crimes unwittingly committed against the child by some mothers: inconsistency, threatenings, objection to his activities because of her neurotic fears, refusal of reasonable requests, ignoring his efforts to be pleasing, breaking promises, quarreling over trivials, transferring her own anxieties, discussing him before others, embarrassing, neglecting, bribing, lying, shielding him from the consequences of his own acts, comparing unfavorably . . . inculcating a dishonest, hypocritical philosophy of life.[1] These are hard words, but any minister,

[1] *Love Against Hate* (New York: Harcourt, Brace & Co., 1942), p. 30.

teacher, army officer, or judge who deals with sons knows they are true words. Would you like to guard against these crimes of smother-hood? I give you some books to read and some guides to keep.

SOME BOOKS

Their Mother's Sons, Edward A. Strecker.
Love Against Hate, Karl Menninger.
Christian Nurture, Horace Bushnell.

SOME GUIDES TO FOLLOW

Thou shalt not be inconsistent in order to keep him close.

Thou shalt not threaten in order to gain thy way.

Thou shalt not transfer thine own neurotic fears in order to control him.

Thou shalt not break promises in order to subdue him.

Thou shalt not quarrel over trivialities to keep the upper hand.

Thou shalt not bribe him to do what is right.

Thou shalt neither lie to him nor for him.

Nor shalt thou shield him in any other way from the consequences of his own acts.

Thou shalt neither embarrass, neglect, compare, nor tattle in order to dominate him.

Thou shalt *wean* thy son!

And the last is the greatest of these. Dr. Strecker puts it plainly: Weaning is as much a part of motherhood as nursing. Taking away is as important as giving. Rejecting and emancipating are as significant as clinging. For, "the child who has known nothing but protection and has only learned to take and not to give has been sadly defrauded by his mother—so badly cheated that it would have been better if he had never been born."

For Pete's Sake

THE LETTERS I HAVE GIVE ME GROUND FOR SAYING THAT NOT ALL the smothering that goes on is the mother's fault. Much of it is the *son's*. For Pete's sake, then, we must face his obligation to help mother be mother.

Pete, you have an obligation too. In plain talk, it is to help her turn you loose by becoming one she can afford to turn loose. Further, you have an obligation to see that she retains all the joy and satisfaction from your relationship that a mother can have.

The other day I heard a foolish kid say a fool thing expressive of a fool attitude. I don't know how prevalent it is, but I jumped clear through when I heard it: "I didn't ask to be born"—and the implication was that since he hadn't and was here through no will of his own, his parents could just by-gosh take care of him, and were obligated to provide all that other kids were getting! For Pete's sake!

The shoes is on the other foot! She didn't *have* to have you. And regardless of all you think you know, she was like 999 of the 1,000 in that she desperately wanted you to be born—you are born of her desire, for it is her desire that gives you the chance to be, much less to become. This basic recognition of the obligation of sons to mothers is fundamental to all right relationship, conduct, morals, and growth. *The growing son is under a debt he cannot pay in full, an obligation he cannot meet, to the one who wanted him and bore him and has endured him.*

It is true that by her willingness to have you she accepted the obligations that go with having sons. But those obligations never included the continuation indefinitely of that pampering, infantile, puerilism some sons take as a right of inheritance.

She did accept the obligation—maybe *too* well. And now you

are under the obligation of a debt you cannot pay to help her release herself from you—and you from her.

In accomplishing the psychological release of completely weaning a son—in the growing process of separation from the womb that asked to bear you—and recognizing the debt you cannot pay that gave you *existence, there are some things she deserves to have from you and with you.*

She deserves the privileges of a growing friendship with you. This is one of the rarest accomplishments I know. Not many sons have sense enough to cultivate a friendship with their own mother. It's taken for granted, but it is not necessarily there— usually it is not there. For, you see, in friendship there can be no excessive domination of either by either. The essence of friendship is *mutuality*—of respect and of confidence. If there is a *friendship* between Pete and his mother, it's almost prima-facie evidence that there is a growing release for both Pete and his mother. She deserves it, and you need it. It's your best way of helping her release you. It takes the place, gradually, of the grasping desire to hold your hand to protect you in your crossings of the busy streets of young adulthood. Friendship sublimates grasping into a sharing—and makes you free!

She deserves the release that can be brought to her only by knowledge of your circumstances and whereabouts. She deserves to know essentially *where you are.* There is no valid way she can release herself from responsibility for your moral and physical welfare. Because she cannot be free of this responsibility, she cannot be rid of concern; she has fears for you—every normal mother does. She deserves to have these fears allayed and her concern satisfied by knowing where you are. I don't say you must not make your own plans; but I do say there's always a telephone, or ought to be. Listen, Pete, the difference this makes is tremendous! It will free you as little else can. It stops that floor-pacing and anxiety-ridden waiting she does. A phone call stops her awful feelings of insecurity—she knows you have changed your plans, have been delayed, have her peace of mind in heart, and she learns to trust and turn you loose. Let her know where you are.

She deserves the further privileges of a confidential relationship even beyond friendship. There are areas where you must always be willing to become little boy for the moment in order that there may continue to be more areas where you are man. There are things you will not want to share with anyone. But *if you will take the initiative in sharing what you can, you will be amazed at how much you are not asked to share.* Have you ever heard of "snooping" mothers? They read letters addressed to you, they overhear conversations, they spy and seek out tidbits of information—Why? Because they have been denied the privilege of mutual confidences—and are starving for it. It grows until they can't learn to trust or release. You must meet this at an entirely different level by volunteering the confidences she *has* to have in order to feel you are still hers, and you achieve as wide an area of freedom as you can use by satisfying her basic urge at a controllable level. For Pete's sake, share confidences with her—or her hunger becomes a fever of desperation and you are hemmed in.

She deserves *dependability* from you. What a sorry son you are if the only way you can be free of her is to lie to her. It's your obligation to see that you never gain a point or escape an issue by lying or deception.

A friend of mine had a call late one night at his church office. The mother wanted to speak to her son. When told that her son was not there, that no one but the pastor was there, or had been there, she was highly incensed—the preacher just didn't know what was going on around there! Of course her son was there! It just never entered her mind that she had a little liar on her hands who had learned to avoid issues by using her obvious approval of certain activities to cloak his participation in things she would not have believed. It's better to have her disapproval than to submit her to the shock of learning she has a liar for a son. Any mother deserves a son who will not lie to gain a point or escape an issue. Any son once caught in a lie to gain his way can never expect to know the freedom a dependable son can always know.

The grandest Son of all sons claimed that honest disobedience that obeys is better than lying obedience that disobeys. Once he illustrated this by saying: "A man had two sons; and he went to the first and said, 'Son, go and work in the vineyard today.' And he answered, 'I will not'; but afterward he repented and went. And he went to the second and said the same; and he answered, 'I go, sir,' but did not go. Which of the two did the will of his father?" (Matt. 21:28-31 R.S.V.)

Would you like a guarantee? I can guarantee that a measure of release, satisfaction, mutual enjoyment, and arriving maturity for *any* son—freedom he has not dreamed *his* mother could give—will follow his honest commitment to the four principles outlined. Try it and see! For Pete's sake!

The Mature Son

SO MANY MOTHERS SEEM TO WANT SO MANY THINGS FOR AND from their sons. Sometimes mothers want accomplishment; always they would welcome standing, advancement, recognition, achievement. It helps if a mother knows what she wants. But it helps more if what she wants for her son is only incidental to his real maturity. It helps when what she expects is only a way station on the road to something more valuable than achievement. I think that is what my mother had in mind when, after I had spent six years of hard work in graduate school, she came to see me receive my doctor's degree. I was really pretty proud—and after the ceremonies were over, my major professor spoke to Mother and said, "I suppose you are very proud." "Oh, no," she said, "I expected it!" And as my foolish pride began to ooze under my silly little mortarboard hat, I had the feeling she *expected* far more than a mere degree.

Perhaps that's the best way to get it—but what should a mother expect from and spend herself to make possible *in* her son? What is a mature son? Degrees, jobs, income, education, right marriage? Not at all, hardly, not even partly. The components of real maturity are far less tangible and far more important than these things.

I struggled long at how to describe the mature son. I knew the characteristics of maturity to be personal and spiritual, but I was not sure I could say them clearly. Then came to my desk an issue of *Scouting,* a magazine for scout leaders, which contained all the help I could use—an article on mental health by the famous William C. Menninger, director of the Menninger Foundation and chief consultant in psychiatry to the Surgeon General. In his article Brigadier General Menninger uses eight characteristics to describe mental health and how scouting contributes to them. With Dr. Menninger's kind permission I am using his eight characteristics of the mentally healthy boy to give my own picture of *the mature son.*

What marks out your son as mature, on the road to full, helpful, healthy life? What should you expect for him and from him to help him achieve maturity? What should characterize his everyday life if he is a mature son?

He can deal constructively with reality, even at its worst. The "end of the world" doesn't come for the mature son. He does not run from fears; he faces his own failures; he works at his own problems; he lives with his disappointments without becoming impossible to live with. His morale can absorb defeat; he can try again; not invulnerable to grief, he leans on no illusions about his own charmed security, but sees whatever comes as it is. He never turns his back on the situation as it is—he goes to work, to fix it if it's bad, and to enjoy it when it's good.

He can find greater satisfaction in giving than in getting. He has been weaned. Life is no longer a matter of taking in—it now involves giving out. The "I" is not central to his universe. He has a "Thou"—and has learned to blend his needs and his gifts with the needs and gifts of others until there are many groups of whom he says, "We." He can belong to a team, a family, a class, a gang—and belongs happily because he is no longer rival to all others for a place to suckle his own ego. He learned somewhere to belong.

He is relatively free from tensions and anxieties. Thus far in life he has always been able, sooner or later, hardly or easily, to *work* through his pressures. He "hears a robin singing, the clouds will soon roll by," at least enough to keep him from brooding over exams he has already flunked, girls he has already lost, and challenges he never could have won. He does not carry anxieties because he has not been taught to love himself so much that he can't forgive himself, nor to love himself so little that he can only despise himself. Though caught in occasional and momentary anxieties, he has friends, a family, and parents with whom these things can be shared—though the problems are still his own.

He can get along with others consistently, with mutual satisfac-

tion and helpfulness. The key word here is "consistently." Most of us can get along occasionally, or even most of the time. The mature son is always in a changing set of situations, and as long as he is alive he is himself a changing "situation." But consistently he meets changing demands with a changing personality and without *clash.* Only rarely is there real occasion for anything except mutual satisfaction and helpfulness. In the world of business it is particularly interesting to watch those immature sons who have some sort of disagreement or estrangement over fully half of their "deals," contacts, and contracts. It is equally interesting to watch how some things just flow on by the mature son.

He can accept frustration for some future gain. The most painful immaturities collect here in otherwise competent, reasonably mature persons. This is a key area. The mature son is not kept from his present work by the thought or dream or anticipation of the unrealized future. He has learned that NOW is sometimes a naughty word—or an impossible one. He doesn't have to have his future now. He can work for it, earn it, deserve it. Short cuts kill more drivers, and he knows it. The mature son will let time *help* him convince the girl, or the boss, or the customer. Meanwhile he's at work!

He has learned to profit by experience. Hegel used to say, "The only lesson learned from history is that no one ever learned anything from history." But the mature son does not fail to learn from his own experience. In his own business? He remembers from a boyhood paper route how slim the margin of profit really is—and watches his overhead. He remembers the weaknesses and the faults that manhood will not remove unless he recognizes and works at improving them. He can even learn from his successes. He can learn from the failures and victories of others. Experience grows as the teacher—and every day he profits from her teachings.

He can direct his hostile instincts into constructive channels.
Yes, even the mature son has hostile instincts. They are born
in him and serve a purpose of self-preservation. Animals have
the same. I watched my usually well-mannered saddle horse
turn into a rushing, charging, wild thing when a colt he had
forgotten was brought back to the pasture—the young horse was
a threat to his position. And the smarter the animal the more
numerous and powerful these hostile instincts. Man *has* to learn
to control, regulate, and sublimate his hostilities or they will
invariably wreck him. The mature son has learned to oppose
wrong without hating *persons.* I remember that my distinguished
predecessor, W. R. White, was once involved in a campaign
opposing the legalization of certain gambling attractions in
Texas. At the end of a particularly warm session before a legisla-
tive committee, the leader of the interests favoring the contested
legislation came around the table to say that he hoped he might
have a chance sometime to vote for Dr. White for governor. In
other words, two mature men had been able to fight out an
issue without hating each other.

He has the capacity to love. The most pathetic grown men I
see are those who have never learned to love. Dr. Menninger
indicates that the largest group of mentally ill patients in
hospitals never learned to love. The absence of ability to love is
one of *the* marks of dangerous immaturity; strong ability to love
is *the* indicator of maturity. The mature man usually will have
found during his boyhood that there are ideals, friends, institutions, communities, people, that he can learn to love. The most
mature of all the sons of men and of God taught us supremely
that this is the mark of spiritual maturity: "By this shall all men
know that ye are my disciples, if ye have love. . . ."

Mamma's Worst Baby

HOW DOES IT HAPPEN THAT WOMEN ARE AS YOU KNOW THEM? There's a character in the famous novel *Adam Bede* who says, "The Lord made 'em to match the men!"

How does it happen that an otherwise stalwart husband-father is frequently mamma's worst baby?

The answer as to how it happens is fairly simple. The cure is a bit more complex—if there is such a thing as cure from such a malady.

To begin with, his earliest years were marked by lack of the right kind of mothering—the kind that produces both security and something of independence. When his mother had finished off her mothering and the wife got him, he was still dangling on the bluff of emotional immaturity—unable to climb up to real maturity or to revert to real infancy. He reached out desperately for his new wife, to make her mother him. But she was more mature, or her attention was diverted, or she was preoccupied with other plans for him, and so for the time being she escaped becoming his emotional mother.

But his problem still exists, more acutely than ever, and with the years he finds himself still seeking the *maternal* affection of his wife. Children come, the wife's true maternal love spills over them, and the husband resents it—he has become rival to his own children for the maternal affection of his wife.

Unsuccessful in vying with his children for his wife's maternal love, the husband may now, and frequently does, become a momish substitute himself. As Strecker puts it, he is "mom in pants." He hovers and smothers. He clucks like an old hen and obviously would hatch something if he could. It's the only sop his ego can find—he will become to his children what his wife has refused to become to him—a smotherer. Needless to say, as his husband-lover-father values decrease, his nuisance value increases. He even asserts his *maleness,* using childish methods, and by the same methods gets his required attention. Added up, it makes him mamma's worst baby.

There are five basic techniques—any one of which, or any combination of which, is unconditionally guaranteed to make a full-fledged baby out of any interested husband who will pursue his advantages assiduously.

He can attempt to secure the maternal concern of his wife by *alienating the children from their mother.* If there is to be any punishment *he* never does it; and what discipline is attempted by the mother can be quite easily blown up by this indulgent, considerate, un-co-operative rival. Nothing will hold against such: allowances, prohibitions, punishment, rules, requirements, discipline, work—all restrictions can be circumvented by this torpedo expert who makes mother to be the grim moralist; and he turns out to be the one to whom the little children run for comfort, indulgence, and maternal affection. He uses certain comforting nuances of voice—"Oh well, honey, that's just the way Mother is; we won't worry about it. Want some gum?" Or he needles the mother into displays of temper, fatigue, disgust. Frequently he actually woos his own children in a kind of psychological seduction—and receives from his own adolescent daughters the maternal affection he has craved from his wife and which they should have been allowed to hold in reserve for their own children. The father gloats in it; and across the years I have known husbands *and* children to be starved for what was still given by a wife and mother to that father who began to rob her years before!

The second basic technique is less complex and almost as effective as the first. It has to do with *the man and his money.* A baby-husband can use the family income in either of two extreme ways to achieve his status as mamma's most needy baby.

He can keep all of it; give her none of it to control, use, or disburse. This asserts his maleness, but it also gets attention—all he can use. Even lunchroom money for the children has to be wheedled from him; under guise of being male and businesslike, every penny of grocery and household funds is doled out; and to buy clothing requires a special act of the legislature and a constitutional amendment. What he craves is not the money— he is not really penurious—he just wants attention, and gets it. The other extreme may be just as effective. By this modification of the old money technique, he gives her all of it. Mother becomes financier, bookkeeper, banker, and manager. His satisfaction comes from the chance he gets to express dependence on her. He gets a lift from successfully wheedling out of her little bits of money, just as he once was successful in working his boyhood mother for candy or whatever he wanted. This is a highly recommended technique—widely used and very successful at making babies out of husbands.

Our third basic technique for becoming mamma's worst baby is really simple—quite easy, in fact—and requires virtually no elaboration. It's the tried and true weapon of *jealousy*. It's used not only on the children, it works just as well everywhere else. Direct it against all your wife's friends—male and female—all her activities, all clubs, all church work, all interests—music, drama, art, sewing, flowers—everything! And one by one she will drop them all to save your feelings, and instead will give you the infantile cuddling you are craving psychologically— maybe she will.

The fourth technique will also work, alone or in combination with numbers three, two, or one. It's the way of *humiliation*. Of course it works best in a crowd and is quite simple in operation. You just wait until she is enjoying herself and some deserved attention, then remind her, by anecdote or remark or jest, of how inadequate she really is—say about making change, or bill paying, or cake baking, or some stupid something or other. This dampens the feathers—is positively soaking in effect when used often and loudly enough. It asserts your superiority, it sends her to your side where she belongs, and forces her to seek her satisfaction in you —that is to say, it reminds her that, after all, you are her baby.

And the last is, in many ways, the most effective of all known techniques for holding one's status as the worst baby mamma has. Its studied application to the situation will positively produce results. This is the technique of *physical dependency*. Hypochondriacs, medicine-chest hounds, and all self-diagnosticians know this technique best. To use it with real finesse calls for artistry. One learns to suffer in silence, sniffle surreptitiously, cough discreetly, glance accusingly, and groan almost inaudibly. As one writer puts it, there is a terrific difference in volume between the cautious groans of the habitual dependent and the surprised bull-like roar of the normal husband in pain. It is in this last area of dependency that the most effective holding action can be maintained. A man can be an infant for years this way.

Now these are all techniques of standard procedure, tested and certified to produce results. Faithfully used they will make a baby of any kind of husband. But what are the counter-techniques? What can the wife do to make her husband grow up?

Frankly, I don't know the cure; I just see the disease. The only suggestions I could make would be much like a cure for the common cold—more of a disinfectant than a therapeutic. But I'll give you mothers all I know: Recognize the problem—and be sure it is the problem—don't falsely accuse. If positive this is the problem, try to talk it out into the open. But remember you are dealing with a little child, so do everything else you know to do without increasing his dependency and making him an even younger baby. Wait as long as you can—ten, twenty, thirty years—and if he still won't grow up, then do as someone suggests, write a note, pin it to his coat, and send him back to his mother. Maybe I could help write the note:

My dear Mother-in-law:

Attached to this note find you infant son. I have tried —— years to help him grow up, but you beat me to him, and you are all he needs. So I send him back to you, just like I got him.

                                            Faithfully yours,
                                            Would-be-Wife

P.S. He eats most anything, provided it's like you fix it.

When Son Takes a Wife

ONE OF THE MOST CRITICAL AREAS OF THE MOTHER-SON RELA-
tionship is entered when the grown-up son takes himself a wife. This is potentially a troubled and emotionally storm-tossed area because not only has a rival to the mother's affections entered the arena—she has been successful! Another female has carried him off. The center of his world has changed—a new queen, new laws, new schemes of value, new diversions, new goals, and other ambitions.

Right here—at the point where a new queen enters—there is more unshirted misery, more unadulterated confusion, more crosscurrents of ill will, more frustration, and more ridiculously unnecessary heartbreak than at any other single point of adjustment which the mother-son relationship has to pass. Sometimes she just won't let him go.

The things I hear:

"*She* isn't good for him."

"*She* is so extravagant, and poor Tom works so hard."

"*She* neglects my precious grandchildren."

"*She* is an only child and spoiled!"

"*She* wasn't reared as I reared mine!"

"*She* turns him against me—and the children too."

"*Her* family certainly isn't much."

"*Her* family has too much."

"He's a good boy and works so hard."

But you never hear her talk like this:

"*I* guess *I* spoiled my son for anyone else."

"*I* failed to teach him self-control and self-discipline."

"*I* made him selfish."

"*My* son is at fault."

It is at this crossroads in life that mothers are frequently most blind. Sometimes the only solution is geographical instead of psychological. It is right here that the three great characteristics of the smothering mother do the most damage: jealousy, meddlesomeness, and immaturity.

Jealousy arises out of the possessiveness of mother love that hates to wean the son. Jealousy will not share any throne with the younger queen. Jealousy picks out weaknesses, seeks for flaws, asks for the hurt that will feed new jealousies. Jealousy determines to remain the "object of affection" at all costs, and sometimes is able to keep the *new* affection from developing.

Meddlesomeness is born and matured in the same cauldron of perverted possessiveness. It is so determined to *own in full* that it peeps, tiptoes, snoops, exposes, sniffs, and probes until it has at the tip of its tongue every secret, every sacred hope, each heartbeat. Meddlesome Mattie, we call her. She is so sure of her own position, skills, and wisdom, that she cannot rest until she is matriarch. Meddlesomeness respects no lock, no seal, no door; it knows every keyhole, crevice, and windowpane. Curious, avidly grasping, she is the would-be decider, midwife to every idea, and purse holder to every dream the young couple share.

Immaturity, the third of the witches, is seasoned in the same brew, molded of the same perverted obsession with one's self as center. But immaturity is coy. She flirts for facts, hints, teases, speaks archly, patronizingly, condescendingly; comes to chew and departs to eschew; can neither share nor spare; gloats inwardly at any breach, weeps outwardly in pretense of concern. Immaturity seeks only the reproduction and justification of its own kind in the young marriage. Immaturity would make its own mistakes the norm. Immaturity—at its best—is witchy.

And it can happen to the best of sons in the "best" of families. The first time I saw him, his native self-confidence, dignity, competency, impressed me. Spare built, with level gray eyes, calm looking—it was a comfort to have a pilot who looked like that when a flight could get rough. Eagle scout, an air-force fighter pilot, then squadron leader, for years now he had been a highly successful operator of the most independent and most dangerous business a man can follow. Sane, steady, devout father and husband that he is, he told me once that not even his years of self-reliance could break the silver cord. And when his marriage was very young: "I just had to get completely away from Mother—she was ruining it!"

Possessive mother! Unless something is done to end this assumption of rights, powers, and influences within your son's marriage, there are only three alternatives discernible to me:

By marring and even completely wrecking his marriage, you will succeed in your effort to return your son to his little-boy status. You will destroy your rival, and he'll be home again—but he'll not be the same.

Or, he will have sense enough to exclude you—cut you off, drop you—in the interest of the preservation of his own home, his own family, his own queen.

Or, you will go on in a miserable mixture of hurt feelings, unhappy holidays, thwarted hopes, dislike, frustration, enmity, and quarreling.

Son, be grown up about your marriage. Establish the right of eminent domain. Whose home is it? If it's yours and your wife's, she has prior right to consideration. In being a husband, don't forget your sonship. Go to see your mother—alone, sometimes. Make arrangements that include her. Head off interferences and troubles before they have time to arise. Don't tell your mother things you keep from your wife. Don't cry and complain to her. Don't make comparisons. Make a place for her in your family life—but don't make a matriarch or a martyr of her. If nothing you can do works—move! Love her from a distance.

Mother, be smart—you have already done about all the good or bad you can do for him. Quit trying to live your own life over in theirs. Let memory do it for you. And even if they make the same mistakes, they have a right to them too. Recognize the prior rights of another. He has obligations now. It's for "this cause" that the Scriptures say a man must *leave* his father and mother. Remember your own opportunity, your own husband, your own chance to have what you haven't had for years—uninterrupted communion and life with the one you said you loved the best and married long ago. He needs you now and you need him.

Mother's Day

WE DESCENDED ON HER YESTERDAY—WAVING THREE TO FIVE TONS OF assorted candy done up in gift boxes; four thousand gallons, at least, of Apple Blossom toilet water at $1.75 per half-pint; fifty thousand yards of nylon slips, petticoats, and hosiery; fourteen dozen gross of imported fragile blossoms on sticks and little wires and green paper; we descended on her yesterday.

We scattered our belongings all over her clean house; we soiled her guest towels cleaning up the kids; and after we had broken a lamp and spilled an ash tray and torn up the Sunday paper, there was a frenzied marshaling of children and off we went to church. For the first time in a year, we sat, all of us, on one pew, red roses in our lapels, singing, listening, standing, sitting all together.

Finally, the long sermon done, we hurried downtown to stand in line for over an hour, waiting for an inferior dinner (compared with hers). And about three o'clock in the afternoon we set her down at home, kissed her good-by for another year, and —duty done—headed home!

Is there anyone who really thinks this is it? Does anyone suppose this to be the way of the best kind of son? Does someone believe this to be what she really wants?

To have you come around on a certain day because everyone does it; to have you sit with her in church because it's what you think she wants; to stand in line for a dinner she may or may not want; to get all her attention from you on a day in May when we all do it—is this it? I think not.

She wants you not to take her for granted. She wants you to think of her and know her as a *person*. A person who has feelings, emotions, memories, desires. She is tired of being a function, a symbol, an official in your life. Or worse still, you may have made of her a baby sitter, an extra helper, a hired hand without pay, a refuge, an extra guest room when you are crowded, an escape valve; but she wants to be person, not just mother, who doesn't mind because she isn't going anywhere anyhow.

She wants to know how you are doing. She needs evidence that you care that she wants to know how you do. She desires *communication*. Sometimes she needs to talk to you or hear from you just because you want to talk to *her*. She ought to know that though you are grown now, you still know times of homesickness. She deserves to hear from you and of you because you want her to know. She has given you up—but not as if you were dead; she craves communication. No distance can excuse the failure to provide it; no busy life can offset this obligation of sonship.

She wants no season of sporadic attention, followed by a long, wide barrenness. She desires *constancy*. What a man owes the right kind of mother requires a lifetime to express; it bears repetition. The constancy she gives deserves answer in its own terms. There is no possible seasonal attention that can make up for the intimacy of constantly expressed affection. She doesn't want you to live with her; she just wants a steadiness of affection, and this requires expression. There are a thousand ways to say it, but extravagant attention one day of the year isn't one of them. She needs constancy.

What mother fails to appreciate having her family with her at worship?—but that is not what she wants in full. She wants your worship to be for your own sake, because of your own recognition of your needs, not hers. Long ago she recognized her need for power outside herself. Now she would prefer your presence in your own house of worship on the basis of your own desire to be there and as expression of the *character* growing within you. She wants character that reveals itself in honest worship of God, not holiday attendance as a favor.

To expand this idea further, along with character, she wants *maturity*. Sure it's fun for her to have you come around and be kids again for a day, but her long-range desires include morality and religious faith on a real basis. No real mother is prouder of anything than of the integrity of life and faith her sons develop.

On the physical level, she loves the little things you bring or send, and she never wants to have to have more from you; but she deserves to know her sons can and will take care of any need she has. It would be a comfort to any mother to know that.

She likes Mother's Day—who doesn't? But she needs to be person, in communication with her son, based on the *constancy* of *mature character* that will meet physical needs too.

THE TERRIBLE TEENS

The Gulf Between

THE TEEN-AGE PERIOD, FOR PARENTS AND FOR YOUNGSTERS, IS FEARED, is enjoyed, is so filled by potential that it develops its own tensions; and yet it is a time of magnificent development. What happens to a fine youngster overnight that turns him into a long, gawky fellow whose wrists stick out five or six inches from his cuffs, whose Adam's apple begins to wiggle up and down as he talks, and whose voice runs off into higher registers? He still stumbles over everything in the living room, can be wistful, though at other times he is very belligerent. Sometimes he is quite pensive, but at other times he is very demanding. An extrovert becomes even more outgoing, and one inclined to look inward becomes more subjective. What has happened? A well-known psychologist says that of all the curable illnesses that afflict mankind the hardest to cure and the one most likely to leave mankind under a chronic state of invalidism is *adolescence*. What makes these wonderful years of rapid growth so impossible?

Teen-agers do not confide quickly in one not of their own age group. You may consider yourself quite fortunate if some teen-ager has chosen to confide in you. For this is for all teen-agers a time of real anxiety. They are searching for some kind of certainty to come out of the panic in which they find themselves. It is a time of change so rapid that the average youngster cannot assimilate with poise what is going on in his body, in his life, in his world.

Most teen-agers will counter that anxiety by adopting a kind of rigid conformity. There appears a very righteous sense of standards, even about clothes. The clothing may be particularly disreputable, or five years too old for her, but the important thing is not that it be right according to any reasonable or decent standard; what is important is that her clothing shall conform to what the rest of the kids her age are wearing. In all ways there is a very rigid idea of conformity to the age group. Your teen-ager will measure his father unmercifully, or his mother—or even his friends. He quickly falls in and out of an affectionate relationship with people by the way they fit or fail to fit his pattern of rigid conservatism.

At the same time there are vast physical changes going on in the teen-ager. He has been a sexual creature all his life. It is not that all of a sudden in the early teens he becomes a creature of sex. He has always been that. But now there is a swift maturing of sex. In addition to all these changes of the physical nature going on, he lives now in a time of intense new feeling. Things are either real gone in one direction or they are absolutely hopeless in the other. He lives in a time of anxious self-centering more than at any other time in life, except in real infancy. Life revolves around him, and he lives in a perpetual daydream of fantasy thinking. This explains some of the clumsiness; it explains some of the crazy things he does.

For example, I was refereeing a course in solid geometry in Louisville Boys High School during the first year of the war. Right in the middle of the only course in the curriculum that would have helped him understand the angles he needed to know to become a gunner, a long adolescent on the back row of the class pointed his finger as if it were the snout of a machine gun on one of the big bombers and yelled, "Ack-ack-ack-ack-ack-ack-ack, got him!" He was shooting down a Jap Zero in the Southwest Pacific, eight thousand miles away from solid geometry.

If during the first four or five years of life his parents have induced ideas of guilt about sex and the body processes, in adolescent age that youngster will become more and more reticent. He will not open up freely to his parents about what he thinks and about what he feels. And, further, his fears are changing.

What was once a sort of personal fear now becomes in addition a social fear. He is very afraid of being laughable; he is very afraid of being left out. He even worries some about not having enough money to preserve the position he wishes to maintain in his group. He worries, strangely enough, about failing, about not measuring up. But primarily he is concerned with a fear that arises out of the problems of choosing and being chosen. It is devastating to him not to belong, or not to be picked, or not to be desired.

In the teen ages, bewilderingly enough to both parents, even the best of parents, there appears a great gap. Now there is a weaning process going on, I hope, throughout the boy's life. But at this level there comes a great widening of the gap between parents and teen-agers. They operate according to different systems. The parents have their ideas of what is important, and the youngster has other ideas. They live in different worlds. To the adolescent, his parents become either a social asset or a liability. Either they help him along or they get in his way. And to the parent, the teen-ager becomes something to fear, or an object of jealousy; and quite frequently, certainly, something not to understand.

The parent and the teen-ager normally know the gulf is there. What separates teen-agers and parents? What keeps some parents and their teen-agers together? Or, we might even better ask, What brings separated parents and their teen-agers back together again?

Neither the parent nor the teen-ager is able to accept the fact that the other person is a "people." Parents are people. Adolescents are people. That is, parents are people to the neighbors, and to everybody else, except to adolescents. And teen-agers are people to other teen-agers, and sometimes to other adults, but not to parents.

Parents are creatures, not gods—creatures who respond to fear and are frustrated every day of their lives, who have needs, and who live with guilt. They have been living with their guilts and fears, their needs, and their emotions quite a bit longer than their teen-age children have. This we know, but why cannot teen-agers understand it?

In the case of the teen-ager and his parent, *a relationship has overspread and covered up a fact.* The same thing is true when you ask the question, Why are adolescents not people to their parents? Again, a relationship has overspread and has become more important than a fact. The parental bugaboo seems to be: How can I escape this relationship of authority that I have with my child, in order that I may become in his eyes a person of whom he is fond, with whom he lives at peace, as with himself? That is his problem too. How can he escape enough of the relationship of dependency on his parents to become in the parents' minds a person? In other words, how can these teen-agers and their parents get rid of this conflict in two levels of development?

The answer is begun when we truly see the problem. If in that relationship of parental authority the parent begins to think of himself as a person, he may later be able to think of his daughter or his son as a person like other persons. If parents, because of their authority, expect too much of these people, then it is just as obvious that the youngsters, because of their dependency, are giving too little, and the result is an emotional problem.

When an emotional problem is clearly understood to be an emotional problem, it is no longer an emotion. If you can think about it, understand and isolate it, it ceases to be an emotion. If it is no longer an emotion, it seldom can remain a problem.

A friend of mine came up and slipped me a little envelope. He said it had been a long rough month for him—he didn't know his youngsters realized it, but all the insurance he owned had premiums due; everything that the family was trying to do together had apparently come due all at once, and he didn't know his sons knew anything about it. When he picked up his breakfast plate an envelope was under it: "To Daddy." It had thirty-six dollars in it.

I would like to congratulate that father, not for getting thirty-six dollars—for I doubt if this would solve his problem—but for having a son who knew his father was a person. Because his father was a person, the son could understand his father's problems and fear and anxieties and needs, and put his weight in to help. This makes a family. It eliminates a gap, when youngsters understand that parents are people, and when parents understand that youngsters are people.

Who's Afraid?

SOME OF YOUR PARENTS WILL SAY, "THERE IS NO FEAR IN MY LIFE." But it is a foolish statement, for fear wears many disguises. Among parents, fear will sometimes appear as strength. Sometimes it will appear very subtly as goodness. The strongest expressions of love may be motivated by a kind of fear. While wearing one of these disguises, fear shapes family policies. Fear may be the moving emotion in our setting up certain standards of behavior—not all of them, but certain of them. Fear in our culture will define success and prestige. And certainly fear frequently acts to restrain many creative energies.

The parental fears that affect the teen-ager are the fears that mark parents in the expansive years of life. These are the years when your parents are still thrusting into a job, when they still hope to arrive at some point they have not yet arrived at; the years before they have finished giving up hope for you; the years when their fears arise out of their pressured inability to measure up, to be here, or do this, or arrive at this.

Some of these fears, with which your parents may not mean to enfold you but in which you are involved, are very selfish; and some of them are not selfish. Fear, for example, may keep your parents from trusting your judgment as much as you think you can be trusted. It is fear that makes your parents hold you too tightly. From your point of view this fear in your parents may hinder your development of freedom; it may keep you immature. To the parents it is the fear of the consequence of trusting you if you choose wrongly.

But teen-agers can help these fears in their parents. At the same time, by understanding that fear is a part of the make-up of all persons, they can come to a vital new relationship with parents. It will help you just to know that some of the things your parents fear arise out of love. Don't pass judgment on your parents' fears. You are not in position to do it yet; just recognize that some fears are valid. Fear belongs as much in life as pain. Recognize that some of your parents' fears are valid; and from your own experience as a teen-ager, remember what fear does to people. Remember especially how fear thrusts up the opposite emotion as if fear were not there, thus creating a barricade to hide behind. For example, fear hides behind anger.

If you can remember what fear does to you, and that your parents are people, and that fear is part of their lives too, then maybe you could learn that there are ways in which you can ease your parents' fears. There are ways you could gain a greater amount of stability and freedom and maturity by helping teach your parents release from fear. I know your daddy is hard to teach; I learn very slowly myself, I fear, from my own children. But, by better communication between you and them, you can teach your parents release from fear. You could include them more often in your plan-making. It takes only a moment to call home when you have changed your plans, and if your parents knew you would take pains to communicate any change of your plans, it would make a world of difference in the freedom that could be given you to decide where you were going. You can teach them release from fear by teaching them you can be trusted. For soon enough you must deal with fears of your own.

What do teen-agers fear? And your answer may be, "They don't seem to fear anything." But teeners do have certain specific fears. In spite of appearances, in spite of devil-may-care air, they are not altogether brainless demons. Every teen-ager has moments of caution; but caution rises from his fears.

What do all teen-agers fear? The teeners I know are afraid of being cut off or held back, or not being allowed to thrust on through with their creative life forces to a full development. In a very crude sense certain rodents, squirrels, horses demonstrate this fear when they fight; for the goal is emasculation of a rival. The same thing seems to be true with the human young one. He fears being cut off; he fears being held back; he fears not being allowed to develop. The big threat to his being allowed to develop is parental authority. This stands over him and cuts off his powers. He is afraid his parents may take him over completely.

One of the most painful things to a teen-ager is to have to endure his father or his mother making some sort of protest in his behalf. This is especially objectionable when mother or daddy or some older person has to go and defend, or go in behalf of, or even talk to some of his younger friends about their being a little more kind to junior. A youngster resents this, and it is part of his fear of being cut off. He fears he will not be allowed to arrive himself; he must make his own way; he resents this being cut off by parental authority.

This same fear expresses itself in exaggerated desires to be grown up. This is what the early use of "make-up" means; this is part of the meaning of early dating as it goes in our present culture. It means that youngsters are pressing against that fear of not arriving personally.

There is a second half of the same great fear. The first is personal; this fear is social. Youngsters fear a *social* exorcism. They fear being cut out by their friends, cast off, not accepted. The pressures here are unbelievable, particularly when you get two fears working counter to each other.

Do you think these wild youngsters who tool these hot rods through unbelievable risks are never afraid while they are driving? Of course they are; they just happen to be more afraid of being "chicken." When two fears operate in opposite directions, the youngster will almost invariably give in to the fear of not being received socially. With the gang he must be thought of as a big man. The worst thing that can happen to him, other than outright rejection, is to have his own parents or some friend cut in, in his behalf. This fear of not belonging is a fear that gets first call over timid, fearful parental objections. And it is in this area of belonging to his peers that parents become such drips in the eyes of teen-agers.

Now I said this social fear gets first call over nearly everything in the teen-ager's life, and this is literally true. Because of this, fearful, moral and personal pressures are exerted on teen-agers. In response to this fear of not belonging, a youngster will put a heavy burden on his whole family to provide means for participation in certain social functions that cost money and require a certain kind of dress. And he does this without mercy or compunction. I know youngsters who have paid a fearful moral price to belong to an inferior group because unfair pressures were exerted on them by their own peers. Another most serious problem is the problem of the effect on personal health that comes from the pressures of extra activism, the wild running with which teen-agers nowadays have to live in order to belong.

If a youngster ever understands that it is fear that presses him into this economic strut, or this moral bind, or this health situation, he may develop nerve enough to be his own kind of man.

In the meantime, there are certain countermeasures that I wish every teen-ager could take and use. There ought to be a big area of his life in which he makes his own way. By the same token, every teen-ager once in a while needs to bite off something he can't chew; he needs to fail at something; he needs to lose once in a while. And don't you worry, Mamma or Daddy; he will lose sooner or later. He needs to have to wait for something. But most of all he needs to be a person, a person pushed by fears just like a parent is a person pushed by fears. And when this happens, parent and teen-ager can really know each other. Something happens to the gap between.

You Lose Your Grip

SOME LOSS OF PARENTAL CONTROL OVER TEEN-AGERS IS NATURAL—YOU may expect some loss of grip. The gap belongs; it belongs in life. These youngsters of yours are getting hold of new standards of comparison and measure. They are learning to be obedient to newer authorities. They are in the process of the completion of weaning that should have begun when they were born. How tragic is the failure to wean. Have you ever known an adult in years who must be controlled emotionally as if he were a pre-adolescent? The fact that weaning is sometimes delayed until years after marriage does not alter the fact that separation is desirable—it belongs. You parents who have done your dead level best must not grieve that the intimacy is not as it used to be. Your relationship is undergoing a change; a change is necessary and your young fellow needs opportunity to grow up.

But the gap that brings so much grief to parents and to teen-agers themselves is the hostile kind of thing where there is bad feeling on a continuing basis. This is not normal, though it is common. It is usually the result of a cycle of emotions, fear, guilt, and hostility, one of which is always in control. This means that the family lives in a continual crisis.

Now, I am conscious not only of parents who already face this problem, but also of parents who are creating for themselves that continuing crisis in the future.

If a parent has tried to force his child to learn bodily and emotional control too soon, the three- or four-year-old may know experiences of failure, awful feelings of rage that he cannot control and subdue without harm, and that he cannot get rid of without being hurt. So he is caught in a terrific frustration with his parents because they have tried too quickly to teach him both physical and emotional control.

If a parent has been so stern and rigid in his rule-making that the child never comes to know him as a loving rewarder, or a gracious comforter, or a warm friend, he may have planted before school years the seeds of fear and hatred. The real emotion that relates him to his parents is envy. He envies them their ability to be powerful over someone else. When you see a little four- or five-year-old boy jabbing at a stuffed puppy or tearing up some toy, he may be envying his father's strength and control. Sometimes he is even venting his sense of outrage aroused by his father.

If you are timid and vacillating, if you move very gingerly

into any correction which has to come, your child does not know where the fence is. He never really gets the hang of things morally; he never knows that this is good, and that is not, because it is good at times and bad at other times. Already you have widened the gap that comes in adolescence when the possibilities of harmful action are infinitely greater.

There are those who have bred an angry sense of injustice into their children by their own failures to live anywhere near the level they require of their children. You may hear a young fellow in a tirade against a playmate and you are amazed—his voice, his expression, his inflection, his very diction—it's your voice, your inflection, your diction, your expression. His voice is your voice, and he has acquired an angry sense of injustice out of your failure to measure up to the requirements you have made of him.

Many parents widen this adolescent gap in early years by making absolutely no allowance for slip-ups or failures, no allowance for regression. When this happens, it means that you already have set up an unmercifully rigid relationship with your child, and by the time he is an adolescent he will have learned from you not to tolerate any difference in taste, opinion, background, or customs. The fact that he is not through with crises of this type simply means that he will move over into adulthood as a narrow and prejudiced person.

How do you work at narrowing the gap? You start before adolescence comes, if it isn't already here, and you seek for yourself the kind of maturity toward which you hope your child can grow. You see, not even with adolescence is a youngster through with his parents—he needs his parents to be mature. Most of the problems adolescents have arise from the need of parents themselves to grow up alongside their children. There are ways to demonstrate your own maturity and theirs:

Recognize the "urge to separateness" in teen-agers. Give them room, but for heaven's sake don't take down all the fences. Set up some reasonable minimum standards early. Participate. Participate in school, scouts, sports; participate in social life, recreational life. And in the name of the holy, develop a religion they can respect and a church connection they can enjoy! There are churches where Christians are joyous people, not bored and dull and stiffened through the drabness of the version of the gospel they have heard. Find yourself one and participate. Make teen-agers responsible through some sort of honest work. Never blame outsiders. In these homes that are producing such grand children I have never heard the courts, the police, the children's friends and associates, school officials and teachers, scoutmasters, coaches, or anyone else blamed for the misbehavior of their own children. And the last, never let them see you fail to face a responsibility squarely. How awful if you squirm and dodge in the face of your own burdens! And it is even worse if they see you dodging and squirming to help them evade their responsibilities. Whatever it is, from bankruptcy to a flunked course, face it straight and see the gap narrow.

Pressures That Hurt

FROM ANCHORAGE, ALASKA, CAME A LETTER A WHILE AGO FROM ONE I have found to be a very brave and very powerful young man. For some years now he has been stretched out by dog sled, plane, and automobile along a front of Christian service too vast for any man. Now that the pressures of all the things he cannot do have piled up around him, there is almost a frantic note as he writes, *"I must learn to walk through life without being shoved!"*

It's a good goal for anyone especially for teen-agers. Do you know anyone more shoved than these? Added to the pressures on teen-agers from without, there are the inevitable, natural pressures from within. Frequently these are pressures that hurt.

There is the pressure to belong which arises out of the fear of *not* belonging. This can have unbelievable force in determining behavior and can work incomprehensible harm.

Nor is there any point in flying against this "pressure to belong." It belongs, too, and is part of normal teen-age make-up; it's standard equipment! If it could be measured, I believe no single force in the lives of youngsters exacts a more fearful moral price and takes a higher health toll than this pressure to belong. At this point, the point of health damage and character change, this pressure to belong demands some kind of handling. How can teen-agers see this and control it?

I know about the demand to belong, to be acceptable to one's age group, but I have no formula for giving a youngster a new or even a worthy set of values. Somehow he must learn to see for himself how false are most demands for conformity. If he can see for himself what a false coloration life takes on from the frothy culture to which most of his compeers are adapted; if he can be led to see the tragic, semitragic, and even comic, results of their actions when based on surface values; if he can see for himself how deadly to human destiny is the premature use of creative powers such as sex; if he can sense the abuse of the future, the profanation of prospects that follow when anything high is brought low—he may refuse by himself, on his own judgment, to pay too high a price for belonging.

The argument for health makes little impression on teen-agers.

Most of them have a constitution like a horse, and gastric juices like Irish setters. Most any abuse will be absorbed for a time. Yet this is a factor in the consideration of the damage done by this pressure to belong. There is an inevitable decimation of physical powers from bad diet, hours, and habits.

How can a youngster achieve this independence that will not be shoved away from decency?

He must come to see that it's *fear* that pushes him to belong. He must understand that *values* are involved. If he can achieve a sense of the *future* and of his own responsibility for his own future, he can be expected to show a maturity about what he is willing to allow to shove him around now.

I have a doctor friend whose wife died years ago. He has had the extraordinary pressures of a busy practice plus the demands of the development of two wonderful children. The eldest, a charming young woman, now married and with children, has been one of those especially winsome young people a pastor knows and remembers. "How did you do all this?" I asked. And his answer was a blessing:

"I simply told her all I could of the high function of every part of her, her body and its organs, her mind and personality. Then, I said to her, 'My dear, you have one body and mind, it's all, the only one you will ever be able to use. For God's sake and your own, use this body and spirit for its highest purpose.'" Then he added a powerful tribute when he said, "She always has."

There is a balance for these pressures! When a youngster knows who he is, and that this is all he has, he can balance the pressures to belong against the pressure to realize his highest. There is dignity and stature in it.

The Family Quarrel

ORDINARILY, PARENTS HAVE "TROUBLE" WITH TEEN-AGERS; AND everywhere parents are a "problem" to teen-agers. If you think you are the only one in your area who has difficulty getting along with a teen-ager, or with a parent, you must understand that everybody has trouble, and that all families have moments of disagreement and confusion.

It may be about money, and usually is. It may be about friends, and usually is. It may be about school and dates, and almost always is. But these do not create any continuing disruption in the family. They are more like occasional disagreements among good friends. Don't you mark your teen-ager off because you do not agree with him right now about his friends, or his dates, or his school habits, or his money habits. These problems flare up, but they flare up safely day after day because the parties concerned, the teen-ager and the parent, in the normal home, know way down underneath that they can rely on each other for affection and protection. It is not any more abnormal for children to wrangle for advantage in this day-to-day relationship than it is for puppies in the same litter to try to get the place of advantage. Indeed, it is this very combination of warm affection and violent disagreement that gives growing up its peculiar impact upon parents and children.

If youngsters merely developed to the point that they exploded into maturity instantaneously, the whole world would be like a little section I have heard of in a rural area. The boy is dominated all his life by physical beatings, until the time he thinks he can whip his father with his fists. If he can, they shake hands and the boy goes his way, working on the farm or away from home—he is independent now, and the father admits it. There is something primitive and animal about this, as if the family were a herd of elk. This is not the way in the normal home at all.

Rather, there is a series of *limited* engagements. No *final* encounter is expected. When the youngster has an argument with you, he is trying to gain a limited objective. It is not an all-out offensive to knock out the enemy; he only hopes to win a temporary advantage. He doesn't want to win the whole battle, because if he did he would lack the leadership and protection he honestly wants.

And over what great issues are these temporary battles fought? Many family arguments are over spending money; almost as many concern the work around the house; nearly all families quarrel sometimes over outside activities. At three points, especially, youngsters complain about their parents: they feel an inability to discuss personal problems with their parents; they feel that their parents are delinquent in accepting them as responsible people; they say their parents are guilty of refusing to discuss sex with them openly and freely. Add to these major issues your own list but it will include: the car, dating, choice of friends, how they were getting along in their school work, and questions of privacy.

Among more than 2,000 teen-age boys and girls, 36 per cent of the boys quarrel habitually with their mother, and 40 per cent of the boys quarrel with their father about friends and social life. Forty-two per cent of the girls quarrel with their mother, and 51 per cent of the girls quarrel with their father about their friends and the social life. Thirty out of every 100 boys and 23 out of every 100 girls quarrel with their mother over the way they spend their money and the way they do their work. Thirty-five per cent of the boys and 25 per cent of the girls have quarrels with their father over their money and their work. Six out of every 100 boys quarrel with their mother over what they are going to wear;

but only 1 out of every 100 ever quarrels with his daddy about it. Perhaps his father shares his problems; I don't know. Surprisingly, only 17 out of 100 girls quarrel with their mother over what they are going to wear. In varying percentages this declines until we find that only 8 boys and 3 girls out of each 100 quarrel with their mother over their education and their occupation while 7 and 5 quarrel with their father.[1] The point seems to be that when you get through adding it up, you get 100 per cent of boys and 100 per cent of girls quarreling with their mamma once in a while and quarreling with their daddy once in a while—and vice versa.

Don't mark your family off because there are flare-ups. Don't assume that you have failed as a mother or as a father because you can't always have perfectly peaceful relationships with your children. And don't think you are the only family in your section of the world that has to put up with occasional disagreements. It belongs, so long as underneath there lies the great sense of affection and support.

Twelve thousand youngsters in one western state insisted that they prized most the privilege of living with people whom they loved and liked.[2] This is normal too! I wouldn't worry too much at your house about those occasional flare-ups and disagreements. Everybody has them. It is part of normal personality.

[1] Raymond G. Kuhlen, *The Psychology of Adolescent Development* (New York: Harper & Bros., 1952), p. 567, Table 95.
[2] *Op. cit.*

The Necessary Mask

HAVE YOU EVER WATCHED YOUR YOUNGSTER BEING SOMEONE ELSE IN a crowd of his own age? Maybe you have a teen-age daughter around your house and you come to the breakfast table wondering which one of seven or eight different kinds of people she is going to be today. Perhaps you wonder if you can trust that overgrown lug of yours to do today what he said last night he was going to do, when you know all the time he will probably be doing something entirely different. You wonder why a teen-ager wears a mask most of the time. The answer, in part, lies in the fact that he *has* to—she *has* to pretend to be somebody else; *in order to get you out of their hair*.

It is at this point, the point of unreliability, the point of "untrustworthiness," we adults say, that we most seriously misunderstand our own teen-agers. You notice how your teen-ager can shift gears from a low depressed mood to a high hilarious giggle the moment the telephone rings—or you notice how quickly he can shift from delightful familiarity to cold aloofness when you accidentally invade his privacy. Typically, the adult responds by saying, "This youngster is unreliable; he is unpredictable; you can't tell what he is going to be, or do, or think."

Perhaps you have noticed your teen-ager in some pensive mood, obviously miles from the "corpse" his mind has left. He is dream-thinking; he is someone entirely different; he is living in a fantastic world of unreality. Typically, you try to get him to do something, or to be something, or to focus on some particular job, and he can't! You dare not mention it, but deep down inside you begin to suspect that your youngster is "dumb," or "unresponsive."

These youngsters wear a mask. We can't get behind the mask to where that teen-ager really is. But it is a mistake to think that the young lady knows nothing of sincerity, or is pretentious.

These are mistakes in judgment, for your youngster is not really unreliable; and certainly very few are dumb or unresponsive, or really irresponsible. Not many teen-agers I know are actually shallow.

In reality this quick emotional changing which we think indicates unpredictability and unreliability is the demonstration of emotional flexibility that anyone has to have to stay alive. Even fish—like squid, and crayfish of certain types, and flat flounders—have the fascinating ability to adjust to changes due to stimuli coming out of the situation around them. The human eye, for example, changes its aperture at the rate of one three-thousandths of a second—everything that lives has to develop a flexibility. In human beings there has to appear a kind of emotional ability to change color.

Those who have thought this dreamworld in which teen-agers live is a mark of weakness, or irresponsibility, ought to understand that this kind of living in an unreal world is necessary to the development of emotional maturity. This ability to protect one's self with a facial or physical, or personality difference, this wearing of a mask, is really an attempt to meet what is expected of them in a given situation.

Let me illustrate in a practical way how I have seen it work around the house. You hear your young lady come in after a day at school, bored, tired, frustrated, and covered up with homework; you hear her moan and complain and accuse—you think she is the most hard-pressed one little girl in all the world. She fusses and fumes and is frustrated, and starts this, and can't finish that, and just can't make it; and you think she must have enough work for three or four days. Then someone calls on the telephone, and supper is ready and she gets a good meal inside her, goes into her room, turns on the radio full blast, and in thirty minutes comes breezing out happily saying her home work is all done. And you think: "How on earth could this be? Which situation is true? Did she not have the homework, or is it not done?" You investigate and you find that she had quite a fabulous load of homework; you also find that it is quite creditably done. But you never quite understand the tremendous capacity to change and to produce and put out.

Or, you have a youngster whose route with newspapers is quickly done if he wants to be in a hurry; but at other times it is a dragging, drudging work-thing for him, and he has to have help. The same fellow can catch fourteen innings of baseball late in the evenings, and you would declare to your soul that he is made out of steel springs because here is no lack of energy at all. You are inclined to think at first that the fellow is unreliable, that the young lady just has no judgment about how much work she really has. But this really isn't true at all; it is a quick emotional fluctuation that conserves output of energy for what one really wishes to do.

In the case of emotional maturing through dream thinking and fantasy thinking, this is a kind of social adjustment. Your youngster is not unreliable. This business of being able to project himself into a number of life situations that are unreal helps him in determining what kind of person he is going to be, and it is not so unrelated after all.

That business of wearing a mask—that sweet angelic look he can put on when you know he is full of devilment—he has to wear it. He dares not let you know what he is thinking. You would beat the daylights out of him if you could, so he wears this protective coloration, this camouflage, this appearance of deceit, to keep relations right at home. He wears it as a device to get his way with his younger brother, or his younger sister. He wears it in order to please you, even to the point of sometimes doing what you want him to do. He wears it to seem to accept the authority you hold over him.

Now, you ask, when is the mask off? And when does dreaming go away? And when can I expect this youngster to be truly stable?

When does the mask go off? The teen-ager's mask never goes off until the adult earns the privilege of seeing behind the mask. The adolescent has been so subjected to shifting authority, changing patterns, and emotional frustrations in his own parents, that it is a very difficult thing for a teen-ager to take his mask off with his own father and mother. By calm living, by fair dealing, by understanding love and affection, you have to earn the privilege of seeing behind your own child's mask.

When does dreaming go away? When he is thrilled with his load, when the responsibility he has assumed is such that he feels he is pulling his own weight. When he is gratified at the trust and responsibility of the given moment in the job he has got, he slows up his dreaming about the big things he may take hold of some day and comes in touch with reality.

And when can you expect your teen-ager to begin to show stability? When the heat is on, when he is squarely up against it in a time of crisis, for himself or for the family, he will demonstrate stability, provided he has had something of an example to begin with. If he sees his parents crawl off and evade and twist in the face of things that are unpalatable, he likely will never achieve the stability you want him to have.

Teen-agers wear a mask because they have to. They dream-think because they do not feel responsible in their own situation. They take off the mask when you have earned the privilege of seeing behind it. They quit dreaming when they are thrilled with their load, or in a time of crisis; and suddenly they become adult for a moment and it is delightful to see.

Some Silly Assumptions

HAVE YOU HEARD THAT TODAY'S TEEN-AGERS ARE MUCH WORSE THAN their counterparts of a generation ago? I have heard of sixty specialists in St. Louis who claim this. It is a silly assumption; it is ridiculous for us to claim that teen-agers are infinitely worse. We can't measure the differences anyway. Given the same social conditions that now maintain, your generation or mine would not have been any better. The statement that youngsters are much worse than they used to be is based on two things: a bad memory and an incapacity for seeing the situation as it is.

Many people who do not have teen-age children assume that all teen-agers are involved in all the bad things we read about. This is a silly assumption, too, and is the same kind of stereotyping, of false categorization, that occurs in racism, or in prejudice against some ethnic group, or against particular types such as airmen, or university students, or on and on you might go.

A third silly assumption appears when we assume that the answer to all teen-age problems is really simple: If the parents know where the teen-agers are, and if the kids have to work, the whole thing will be fixed.

If it appears that teen-agers are worse, it could be because the surrounding cultural situation is much more shallow. Individuals are much more vulnerable because they are much less stable. The values we have arrived at in our culture mean that we have built more flimsy fences to be run through. In part, extravagant adolescent behavior is a kind of reaction against our shallow and surface system of values. No one is capable of being more serious or more intent than a normal sixteen-year-old. At this time in his life his values are inclined to be as high as they will ever be; his religious valuations are more sincere; his interest is more genuine, and his rebellion against surface conformity and hypocrisy is also at its highest. I say that instead of youngsters on the whole being much worse, it could be possible that the cultural environment, the situation in which we live, is much more shallow.

The fact that most teen-agers look alike to us does not mean that they are really alike; it means that we are getting old, and we are not sensitive to the distinctions that mark personality. This is but one of many kinds of false stereotyping.

If parents know where their kids are and put them to work, this indeed helps. The fact that I worked ten hours a day unloading steel in the summers had something to do with what I did on summer nights, for there wasn't much energy left for running around. But even though parents know where their children are and that they are involved in work, this is not the whole of the answer. It is not quite so simple.

For much longer periods of time now, teen-agers are tied in a kind of economic vassalage. They are almost totally dependent upon the home and the home's resources and the home's income. Within the home and the society there is such a definite limitation of resource and responsibility that the youngster never quite comes into his own until five or eight years past the time he was expected to come into his own not more than twenty years ago. Again, the answer is not quite so simple any longer, because the scale of values upon which our culture swings, the value level within which most youngsters grow up, is inescapably bad because it is almost incurably materialistic. Youngsters learn from their elders, and from the way we live, that the things that are truly valuable to us are material things. We have ignored great and vast areas of potential within the lives of teen-agers; and this means that we have ignored the development of those areas. So I say the answer is not so simple.

We ought not to assume, without any adequate way of measuring, that teen-agers are worse. We ought not to make the deadly mistake of assuming that all teen-agers are alike, or that the answer is simple. Our whole culture is involved. Not all the trouble that has been reported is juvenile anyhow, unless you raise the age bracket of what you call juvenile.

Point of View

A young friend of mine in Tarrytown has a beautiful collie. Tucky, the collie, frequently crawls in bed with Polly, the friend, and takes a nap. One day Polly's grandmother came in and found them sleeping, both heads on the pillow. "Polly, why don't you push old Tucky off the bed?" And Polly said, "Now Grandmamma, don't you go bothering Tucky; Tucky doesn't know I am not a dog." It depends on your point of view.

Several times we have seen our white cat jump on the TV set in order to watch. Now I suppose lots of animals watch TV, but it is a little unusual for a cat to be a regular TV watcher, the way our cat watches. She jumps on the cabinet, hangs her head over the picture screen and watches it upside down, slapping with her paw at the shadows as they go by. Now whether you are a teen-ager or a pussycat, what you get out of anything depends on your point of view. Puff's TV experience is valid, if you are a cat. The cat watches TV and we watch the cat, and sometimes there is a question as to who gets the most. It depends on your point of view.

The point of view of anything is important. It is particularly important that a parent be able to get the point of view of the teen-ager, and it is critically important that a teen-ager be able to catch the point of view of the parent. When our cat is watching TV from the top of the TV case, looking down over the picture screen and slapping at the shadows with her paw, things are all turned around for her, I think. It may be that she is not there to look at the picture. She may be there just to slap at the shadows. If she is, it really doesn't matter. It depends on her point of view. The point of view changes things. If she is there to watch TV, things are all squared around wrong. They are upside down; they are topsy-turvy. But if she is just there to slap at shadows, things are O.K. I suppose an upside-down shadow is quite as good as a shadow that is right side up.

Your point of view is important; and the point of view changes things. I know of no other way that you can understand anyone whose point of view you cannot catch. This goes all through life, and is the basis of most parent-child disagreements. The adolescent just cannot quite get the point of view of the parent; the parent just can't quite get the point of view of the youngster. This is true in discussions between different types of Christians. This is true between believers and unbelievers. This is true when a man posits his reasons for existence on what he calls knowledge, which is always approximate; and that of some other man who posits his way of life on something which he calls faith, which never is knowledge.

This is particularly true, this point-of-view business—this strange need to catch and know and understand another man's point of view—it is particularly important in all those areas of life where emotion rules primarily.

It is true in politics. Not many people sit down and square away with an issue and come to a rational decision as to where their support will go. This is true in matters involving race. Most of us have been so conditioned through childhood and adulthood that we simply have an emotional reaction instead of making a rational study of a problem. This is especially true in religious matters. We act on the basis of what our emotional mind-sets are; and it is undoubtedly and sometimes painfully true in family life that a certain mind-set, a certain point of view, is expected to characterize the thinking or the vision or the planning or the participation of this child or this parent.

In those areas of life where emotion rules predominantly, it is particularly urgent that, if we are to live together, as families ought to live, we learn to acquire another point of view—any other point of view. For there is an amazing possibility that there may be some truth to some other view. There is an amazing possibility that I may not see the whole picture. There is quite a definite chance that the father may not understand at all that there are sometimes even rational reasons why children are doing some of the things they do, and why they wish to do some of the things they are denied the privilege of doing.

There is no man who is really able to have fellowship, to understand, to get along with his own children, who has not acquired somewhere, somehow, a capacity for seeing other points of view. And as he gets this ability to see other points of view, he finds himself climbing out of his prejudices, out of his provincialisms; he becomes a freer man; he becomes a stronger man; he becomes a more gracious man; he becomes a more attractive fellow; he becomes a much more dearly loved parent. To tell you the truth, the minute he begins to see the amazing possibility that he may not know the whole story, that he may not have the whole picture, that he may not be in possession of all the truth, when the amazing possibility, I say, dawns on him that there may be some validity to some other point of view, he becomes less authoritarian, less an autocrat, less a dominator, and he becomes a participator. When the shocking realization comes to an adult that there is a possibility that he might be mistaken about something, he is already on the road to acquiring that remarkable capacity for thinking from some other point of view.

I have never tried watching TV like our Puff watches it; I am not sure that there is any advantage in watching TV from the top of the set with your neck craned down over the screen, slapping at the shadows as they go by; it may have some advantage, I don't know. Because I haven't tried it yet, perhaps I haven't the right to say whether or not our house cat is getting anything out of TV. Or if I did try it and didn't particularly like it, I am not sure I would still have any reason to say Puff did not get anything from TV. Maybe she is getting it like a cat gets TV; and maybe that youngster at your house is getting a lot of good from a lot of things that you miss simply because you can't quite get his point of view. I expect that it looks all upside down to you at times; but don't make the mistake of assuming that because you have different points of view there is no validity to any other view.

Edge of Adulthood

IT MUST SEEM A LONG ROAD FROM MEREST INFANCY TO THE TIME REAL adulthood comes to your adolescent young people. In fact, for many parents this day never really comes. I know many a grandfather and grandmother tortured and confused with the problems of their own middle-aged youngsters. In every normal home there ought to come a time when all that you have waited for and all that you have poured into these years of nursing and weaning and waiting ought to pay off. Your youngsters ought one day really to come of age. They ought to be adult, and therefore enter into an adult relationship with parents that is normal, and wholesome, and happy.

Now this adulthood for your youngsters may come rather suddenly with some; and it may be approached most gradually, if at all, on the part of other families; and tragically enough, it just never comes for many, many families. Actually, young people have to earn their adulthood. They must, society says, win through to true adulthood. This happens among us almost the same way it has happened for eons among primitive tribes.

With the American Indian tribes, for example, a young fellow a little beyond the age of puberty had to win through by physical torture, endurance, and demonstrations—demonstrations of character, of competency in the religion of his tribe, his right to sit in councils of the tribe, his right to be called a first-line defender of the tribe, his right to be father of a family within the tribe, his right to be a benefice in the provisions the tribe made for its own common welfare. Youngsters grew up in the knowledge that one day they would have to demonstrate judgment, character, skills, ability to survive, ability to endure, and the basic kind of character the tribe required. Sometimes this required days of isolation on a mountainside; sometimes this required a kind of self-torture and loneliness that could end only with the coming of some truly significant vision. But always he entered into the tribe in a series of ceremonies appropriately recognized by proper rites, and he took his place in his tribe as a defender and provider, and as one who would benefit by membership in the tribe and would give his life to the tribal line.

But our youngsters have to earn adulthood too. And there are all kinds of tests, checking-up places, shock places, demonstration places, requirements, episodes on the way to an honest, earned, responsible adulthood. This is the goal of the adolescent, and it is tragic when it is not also the goal for the parents. Our youngsters have to earn their adult status in the community just as definitely as the child of any primitive tribe ever had to demonstrate his. With us it is more gradual. Sometimes it comes a little earlier; sometimes it is delayed altogether.

I suppose the ancient tribes had a way of disposing of those who never quite made it to adulthood. I am sure it was a very rigorous and cruel way; but we are just as cruel and just as rigorous in our society in disposing of those who never quite made it to adulthood. Frequently we just marry each other and go on as little children, living together like little children, creating an inferno—a torture chamber for each other and for ourselves and for our children. This is a crime against nature; it is a crime against reason; it is a crime against God.

Often parents are the greatest obstacle a teen-ager may have in winning his way through to adulthood. Sometimes, someone who has the respect of the family needs to say to a father and a mother: Get out of the way; get off the lid; turn him loose; quit being so fearful; or quit being so jealous; or quit being so possessive; or quit making yourself such a rival; or quit regretting your own lost youth.

Parents are supposed to help children become adults, not pervert them from adulthood. Frequently you run into a situation where a parent makes the mistake of never quite knowing when his judgment and his help are really a limitation and a hindrance. There are parents who just can't quite conceive of there ever being a time when their help would not be needed or welcomed.

At our neighborhood drugstore one day I was hailed by a friend whom I have enjoyed for seven or eight years. Highly skilled in his profession, a man whose family I have known well, and whose children I have enjoyed, he stopped me to tell me of a wonderful thing that was happening in his family. He said it was happening all at once. All of a sudden their eldest, sixteen years old now, became an adult. She just walked into a new kind of relationship. All at once there were jokes they could share; there were stories they could tell; there were things they could laugh about. And they caught themselves, he said—with something of wonder on his face—looking across to that sixteen-year-old daughter as a full equal, a responsible partner, a competent witness, as a full-orbed, openhearted adult ready for whatever life could bring—good or bad and able to take either. This is a delightful thing. This is what we are working for.

For this a man can hardly wait, though he hates to push the time on by so rapidly; he can hardly wait, because now he has a hunch that the same thing is going to happen when his younger one and his still younger one come in the neighborhood of his eldest. He is going to find himself—all of a sudden or gradually —learning how to look straight across to openhearted, fully responsible, competent adults who welcome the continuing love and affection and support and guarantee and security that come long after each is married and has a home of his own. I hope that can happen at your house.